Economic Evaluation of Public Programs

James S. Catterall, *Editor*

NEW DIRECTIONS FOR PROGRAM EVALUATION
A Publication of the Evaluation Research Society
ERNEST R. HOUSE, MARK W. LIPSEY, *Editors-in-Chief*

Number 26, June 1985

Paperback sourcebooks in
The Jossey-Bass Higher Education and
Social and Behavioral Sciences Series

Jossey-Bass Inc., Publishers
San Francisco • Washington • London

James S. Catterall (Ed.).
Economic Evaluation of Public Programs.
New Directions for Program Evaluation, no. 26.
San Francisco: Jossey-Bass, 1985.

New Directions for Program Evaluation Series
A Publication of the Evaluation Research Society
Ernest R. House, Mark W. Lipsey,*Editors-in-Chief*

Copyright © 1985 by Jossey-Bass Inc., Publishers
and
Jossey-Bass Limited

Copyright under International, Pan American, and Universal
Copyright Conventions. All rights reserved. No part of
this issue may be reproduced in any form—except for brief
quotation (not to exceed 500 words) in a review or professional
work—without permission in writing from the publishers.

New Directions for Program Evaluation (publication number
USPS 449-050) is published quarterly by Jossey-Bass Inc.,
Publishers, and is sponsored by the Evaluation Research Society.
Second-class postage rates paid at San Francisco, California,
and at additional mailing offices.

Correspondence:
Subscriptions, single-issue orders, change of address notices, undelivered
copies, and other correspondence should be sent to Subscriptions,
Jossey-Bass Inc., Publishers, 433 California Street, San Francisco,
California 94104.

Editorial correspondence should be sent to the Editor-in-Chief,
Ernest House, CIRCE-270, Education Building, University of Illinois,
Champaign, Ill. 61820.

Library of Congress Catalogue Card Number LC 84-82377
International Standard Serial Number ISSN 0164-7989
International Standard Book Number ISBN 87589-764-9

Cover art by Willi Baum
Manufactured in the United States of America

Ordering Information

The paperback sourcebooks listed below are published quarterly and can be ordered either by subscription or single-copy.

Subscriptions cost $35.00 per year for institutions, agencies, and libraries. Individuals can subscribe at the special rate of $25.00 per year *if payment is by personal check*. (Note that the full rate of $35.00 applies if payment is by institutional check, even if the subscription is designated for an individual.) Standing orders are accepted. Subscriptions normally begin with the first of the four sourcebooks in the current publication year of the series. When ordering, please indicate if you prefer your subscription to begin with the first issue of the *coming* year.

Single copies are available at $8.95 when payment accompanies order, and *all single-copy orders under $25.00 must include payment*. (California, New Jersey, New York, and Washington, D.C., residents please include appropriate sales tax.) For billed orders, cost per copy is $8.95 plus postage and handling. (Prices subject to change without notice.)

Bulk orders (ten or more copies) of any individual sourcebook are available at the following discounted prices: 10-49 copies, $8.05 each; 50-100 copies, $7.15 each; over 100 copies, *inquire*. Sales tax and postage and handling charges apply as for single copy orders.

To ensure correct and prompt delivery, all orders must give either the *name of an individual* or an *official purchase order number*. Please submit your order as follows:

Subscriptions: specify series and year subscription is to begin.
Single Copies: specify sourcebook code (such as, PE8) and first two words of title.

Mail orders for United States and Possessions, Latin America, Canada, Japan, Australia, and New Zealand to:
Jossey-Bass Inc., Publishers
433 California Street
San Francisco, California 94104

Mail orders for all other parts of the world to:
Jossey-Bass Limited
28 Banner Street
London EC1Y 8QE

New Directions for Program Evaluation Series
Ernest R. House, Mark W. Lipsey, *Editors-in-Chief*

PE1 *Exploring Purposes and Dimensions,* Scarvia B. Anderson, Claire D. Coles
PE2 *Evaluating Federally Sponsored Programs,* Charlotte C. Rentz, R. Robert Rentz
PE3 *Monitoring Ongoing Programs,* Donald L. Grant
PE4 *Secondary Analysis,* Robert F. Boruch
PE5 *Utilization of Evaluative Information,* Larry A. Braskamp, Robert D. Brown

PE6 *Measuring the Hard-to-Measure,* Edward H. Loveland
PE7 *Values, Ethics, and Standards in Evaluation,* Robert Perloff, Evelyn Perloff
PE8 *Training Program Evaluators,* Lee Sechrest
PE9 *Assessing and Interpreting Outcomes,* Samuel Ball
PE10 *Evaluation of Complex Systems,* Ronald J. Wooldridge
PE11 *Measuring Effectiveness,* Dan Baugher
PE12 *Federal Efforts to Develop New Evaluation Methods,* Nick L. Smith
PE13 *Field Assessments of Innovative Evaluation Methods,* Nick L. Smith
PE14 *Making Evaluation Research Useful to Congress,* Leonard Saxe, Daniel Koretz
PE15 *Standards for Evaluation Practice,* Peter H. Rossi
PE16 *Applications of Time Series Analysis to Evaluation,* Garlie A. Forehand
PE17 *Stakeholder-Based Evaluation,* Anthony S. Bryk
PE18 *Management and Organization of Program Evaluation,* Robert G. St.Pierre
PE19 *Philosophy of Evaluation,* Ernest R. House
PE20 *Developing Effective Internal Evaluation,* Arnold J. Love
PE21 *Making Effective Use of Mailed Questionnaires,* Daniel C. Lockhart
PE22 *Secondary Analysis of Available Data Bases,* David J. Bowering
PE23 *Evaluating the New Information Technologies,* Jerome Johnston
PE24 *Issues in Data Synthesis,* William H. Yeaton, Paul M. Wortman
PE25 *Culture and Evaluation,* Michael Quinn Patton

Contents

Editor's Notes 1
James S. Catterall

Chapter 1. Choosing Between Retraining and Job Placement Strategies for Displaced Auto Workers: An Economic Analysis 5
Jane Kulik, D. Alton Smith, Ernst W. Stromsdorfer
This chapter analyzes efforts to reemploy displaced workers in the Detroit area between 1980 and 1983 through the Downriver Community Conference Economic Readjustment Program.

Chapter 2. A Design for an Economic Analysis: The Wisconsin Child Support Demonstration 31
Irwin Garfinkel, Thomas Corbett
This chapter outlines a plan for assessing the economic and behavioral effects of alternative child support payment systems proposed for experimentation in Wisconsin counties.

Chapter 3. Economic Transformations of Nonmonetary Benefits in Program Evaluation 53
Stuart S. Nagel
This chapter suggests ways of grappling with the problem of achieving uniform standards of comparison for alternative policy choices entailing differing multiple outcomes.

Chapter 4. Capital Costs in Economic Program Evaluation: The The Case of Mental Health Services 69
Nancy L. Cannon, Thomas McGuire, Barbara Dickey
This chapter illustrates the critical importance and typical underconsideration of capital costs in evaluations of institutional arrangements for the delivery of public services.

Chapter 5. State-Level Evaluation Uses of Cost Analysis: A National Descriptive Survey 83
Nick L. Smith, Jana K. Smith
This chapter describes the models for program cost analysis and the survey documenting the extent of use of cost assessments in educational evaluation.

Chapter 6. Economic Directions for Program Evaluation 97
James S. Catterall
This chapter examines the critical dimensions of economic analysis for program evaluation.

Index 103

Editor's Notes

It may be unfair to portray the worlds of economists and public program evaluators in broad brushstrokes, but some generalizations about the two have nonetheless inspired this *New Directions* sourcebook. We have long known that applied economics and program evaluation embrace common interests that are not fully recognized in their mainstream traditions. We also know from years of working on the interface between the two realms that building meaningful bridges is not an easy task for a number of reasons. A primary purpose of this volume is to do some bridge building.

The common interest that economic analyses and program evaluations share is this: Both seek to optimize organizational or social resource allocation. Much of what evaluators and economists do is ultimately grounded in this rationale, whether they acknowledge it formally or not. The evaluator seeks to determine what sorts of interventions work best when specific goals are sought. Thus, understanding program effects is a primary focus of the program evaluator's activities. The economist works to refine our understanding of relationships between resource use and program effects. Thus, understanding the efficiency implications of alternative intervention strategies is a primary focus of the economist's efforts.

Although education policy analysis is not a central concern of this volume, it provides some helpful illustrations. Evaluators of educational programs have long occupied themselves with discerning the degree to which training or other educational institution–based programs yield their intended or other results. This has led education evaluators to scrutinize concepts of cognitive, attitudinal, and behavioral changes and questions of their measurement. For example, first-grade reading programs are shown to yield certain patterns of gains on achievement tests, counseling programs are shown to influence high school juniors' postgraduation plans in specified ways, and so forth. The knowledge gained in educational program evaluations is useful in the degree to which it benefits decisions made at any of several organizational or societal levels.

Economists suggest that knowledge about the relative degrees of effectiveness of, for instance, alternative reading instruction strategies is necessary for good decision making, but it is not sufficient. Alternative strategies that might attain desired ends are likely to vary in cost. Information about the effectiveness of programs (the results of evaluation) should be combined with information about costs if institutions are to maximize the impact that they can achieve with their finite resources. Economists have contributed to such synthesis by developing cost analysis models, such as cost-benefit, cost-effectiveness, and cost-utility analysis. Economists have contributed to questions of program evaluation in another way by focusing on labor market outcomes of training interventions. Education and training are supported in part because such experiences are thought to promote economic participation by individuals and to enhance the productivity of society in general. Economists have focused on the nature of these outcomes. Implicitly, they have suggested that such outcomes are critical to educational program evaluations.

This sketch says nothing either of the interesting or problematic issues in these fields or of the realms in which researchers or practitioners seeking to expand our ways of knowing and analyzing the relevant phenomena are now active. It does, however, serve to introduce the reader to this *New Directions* sourcebook. In the first paragraph of these editor's notes, I described the mission of this volume as one of bridge building; now I will be more specific.

What kinds of bridges do the contributors to this volume wish to build? We begin with the fact that many of our readers are practicing program evaluation professionals or researchers who focus on issues of program evaluation. Our hope is to provide these readers with meaningful exposure to economics-based models that may be relevant to their work.

Our efforts to provide such information are constrained by two facts. First, the full complement of economic models that are relevant to program evaluation is extensive, and it is impossible to cover them all in a single volume. The alternative—simply cataloguing them—has no practical utility. Second, if my own experience in training educational evaluators in economic reasoning provides any guidance, an intensive how-to methods sourcebook—even one confined to a single subdiscipline, such as cost-effectiveness analysis—is not likely to convince evaluators that what economists have to offer has interest for program evaluation. Besides, a comprehensive range of reasonably clear methodological treatises is currently available.

We chose instead to rely on communication by example. Hence, our approach is somewhat eclectic. First, we offer readers a thorough and detailed report on a recent economics-based evaluation. The study described by Jane Kulik, D. Alton Smith, and Ernst W. Stromsdorfer in Chapter One—an analysis of training programs provided to displaced auto industry workers in the Detroit area—is unique in that it is both exemplary in its own field and understandable to readers with little or no formal training in economics. In Chapter Two, Irwin Garfinkel and Thomas Corbett describe an economics-based design for an evaluation of a program demonstration proposed by Garfinkel. The object of this evaluation is an array of schemes for improving the flow of court-awarded child support payments. The next two chapters take up some methodological issues. The first involves the treatment of multiple and noncommensurable outcomes of programs. It applies directly to both economic and effects-focused evaluations. In Chapter Three, Stuart S. Nagel explores several alternative ways of quantifying or "monetizing" program benefits for the purposes of evaluations. His work suggests ways in which decision maker or other stakeholder values can be used as the basis for appraisals of alternative mixes of unlike outcomes. Nagel's formulations provide some practical relief to those who disdain cost-benefit analyses because there is no satisfactory way of monetizing the nonmonetary benefits of programs. The second methodological issue is equally critical and underattended: the analysis of capital costs in public services. In Chapter Four, Nancy L. Cannon, Thomas McGuire, and Barbara Dickey describe a study based on their current research into public mental health service alternatives. The issue of capital costs has been selected because it is relatively neglected in the literature, because it is critically important to evaluations that consider alternatives to institution-based services or the competing claims of public and private delivery structures, and because capital costs are very substantial when such services as health programs are considered. In Chapter Five, Nick L. Smith and Jana K. Smith present a sketch of cost-analysis models and report on the results of a recent survey into the use of economic evaluation models, particularly of cost analysis perspectives, by evaluators of education programs. The results of this survey suggest that efforts of the sort undertaken here are justified. Finally, in Chapter Six I review the central contributions of the authors and point to an agenda that might extend the directions offered in this sourcebook.

James S. Catterall
Editor

James S. Catterall is assistant professor of educational administration and policy studies in the Graduate School of Education, University of California, Los Angeles.

Riel
 Net
 needs
 no Net
 in we
 retra
 displa

What resulted from our efforts to retrain and reemploy workers whose jobs were lost through reorganization of the American automobile industry during a recent recession?

Choosing Between Retraining and Job Placement Strategies for Displaced Auto Workers: An Economic Analysis

Jane Kulik, D. Alton Smith, Ernst W. Stromsdorfer

To develop information regarding the effectiveness of alternative methods for reemploying displaced workers, the U.S. Department of Labor has funded several pilot projects since 1980. This analysis examines one of the first such projects to receive federal funding: the Downriver Community Conference dislocated worker program, which served laid-off automotive workers in the Detroit metropolitan area. This program operated in two phases between July 1980 and September 1983. The first phase, which operated from July 1980 through September 1981, made services available to approximately 1,500 workers laid off from the BASF and DANA automotive supply plants. The second phase of the program, which continued from November 1981 through September 1983, extended eligibility to workers laid off from the Ford Motor Company Michigan Casting plant and the Firestone Tire and Rubber plant. More than 2,100 workers received Downriver program services during the combined operating periods.

J. S. Catterall (Ed.). *Economic Evaluation of Public Programs.* New Directions for Program Evaluation, no. 26. San Francisco: Jossey-Bass, June 1985.

The largest component of this analysis is an estimation of program impacts on participants' reemployment and earnings. To estimate these impacts, comparison plants were selected from within the Downriver labor market area to provide benchmarks against which program interventions could be measured. These comparison plants were chosen for their similarity to the plants made eligible for program services along a number of dimensions that seemed likely to correlate with workers' reemployment. These dimensions included the plant's previous layoff history, closure date, scale of layoffs, product, and income support benefits for the plant's workforce.

A random sample of approximately 2,600 workers, equally divided between program-eligible and comparison plants, was interviewed in person to obtain information about their employment and income sources for an average of two-and-one-half years after layoff. For those laid off in 1979, almost four years of information were available.

The impact analysis focuses on three characteristics of the reemployment process: the reemployment rate, defined as the fraction of workers ever obtaining employment during the period after layoff; the employment rate, defined as the fraction of period after layoff in which workers were employed; and average weekly earnings during the period after layoff. The first measure is analogous to the placement rates that program operators use to gauge the success of their efforts. The other two measures are more correct summary indicators of program impact. The analysis considers both the net impacts of program training as compared with job search assistance alone. Because of differences in the program over time as well as differences in local economic conditions, the impacts of the two program phases are analyzed separately. Effects are also estimated separately for each program service plant as a means of isolating plant-specific effects.

Program Participation

Before discussing the program's impact on the labor market, we describe the nature of worker participation in this program. The reader should know that these are mature workers with an historically strong and consistent labor force attachment. They are not the typical disadvantaged workers on which the Comprehensive Employment and Training Act (CETA) of 1963 was largely targeted. The strong labor force attachment of these workers should affect the degree and nature of their participation in the program and subsequent program outcomes.

The critical demographic and economic characteristics are these: Dislocated workers eligible for the Downriver program were predominantly male, between the ages of twenty-five and forty-four, married, and with family responsibilities. Close to 60 percent of the program-eligible workers had completed high school or received additional training. These seemingly high levels of educational attainment masked a low literacy level: Some 20 percent of the participants scored below sixth-grade levels on standardized reading and mathematics tests administered by the program. While some of these workers could be assisted by a refresher course, most were lacking in these basic skills. This made it difficult either to market them to employers or to place them in classroom training programs. Program-eligible workers were typically experienced production workers with more than ten years of experience on the layoff job who earned approximately $9 per hour. This combination of extensive work experience and high wages before layoff suggested that one of the first tasks for program staff would be to convince these workers to lower their reservation wage. At the same time, staff established an explicit goal of minimizing earnings loss for participating workers. Participation was high across both phases of the program, averaging close to 50 percent. This high participation rate can be attributed to two factors: first, the explicit targeting of program services to workers laid off from particular plants and, second, the active involvement of affected employers and unions in outreach and reemployment efforts. Younger workers, better-educated workers, and workers with low wages before layoff were most likely to participate in the program. Participation rates declined steadily with age and level of firm-specific work experience. On average, workers waited approximately sixteen weeks after their layoff before enrolling in the program. This observed waiting time suggests that workers searched unsuccessfully for new jobs for some time before seeking assistance. Given that those who joined the program appeared, at least based on their demographic and labor market characteristics, to be those for whom services could be expected to have some impact, the question of whether they were drawn into the program quickly enough to receive maximum benefits becomes a serious issue.

Downriver Design Elements Relevant to Labor Market Outcomes

Given the characteristics of the dislocated workers who were made eligible for program services, five attributes of the Downriver program model are important when we consider the manner and extent of potential impact on labor market outcomes. First, since program participants were experienced production workers with solid work habits, Downriver staff placed overriding emphasis on finding jobs for these individuals. Workers who needed supportive services (including financial and personal counseling or medical assistance) were referred to a network of community agencies. No supportive services were provided directly by the program. Second, a mandatory two-week assessment and job search training sequence was a prerequisite for receipt of additional program services. Participants were required to take standard aptitude tests and to participate in job search training. This sequencing of services served two purposes: It ensured that only those who were committed to reemployment received services, and it helped program staff to gauge how many workers were likely to require retraining in order to become reemployed. Third, for participants interested in retraining, an assessment process was established that included a review of the individual's test scores and performance in the job search workshop. This assessment was designed to screen out those interested in classroom training but lacking either the aptitude (measured by test scores) or the motivation (measured by attendance and participation in the workshops) to succeed. Fourth, a full menu of program services was established that involved job search assistance and job development, classroom and on-the-job retraining, and relocation assistance. With the exception of job development, service delivery was contracted out to existing providers using performance-based contracts or, at minimum, careful monitoring of outputs. Program staff avoided reinventing the wheel by making strategic modifications to existing curricula or programs. Fifth, in developing training programs, the emphasis was placed on short-term, technically oriented courses that met employers' needs. Training curricula were reviewed by employer committees to assess the degree to which the courses would yield trained workers who could fill entry-level positions in growing fields. To ensure that program placement staff had an opportunity to work with trainees once their schooling was completed, staff attempted to compress programs into a six- to eight-month period.

Response to the services made available by the Downriver program sheds some light on the reemployment needs of the dislocated workers. About 60 percent of the participants received some form of retraining. Twenty-eight percent enrolled in existing degree programs offered by local educational institutions, and another 25 percent took part in class-size programs developed by Downriver staff. The remaining trainees enrolled in on-the-job training positions. Younger and better-educated workers were most likely to receive training. During the first phase of program operations, participants were enrolled in training for an average of eight months. In the second phase of the program, high dropout rates caused the training period to be shortened by approximately two months. Slight use was made of the program's relocation and out-of-area job search assistance components. Only 8 percent of the participants relocated, and approximately 20 percent of those who did returned to the Downriver area. Staff were careful to point out, however, that they gave very little publicity to the program's relocation services, perceiving this as a high-risk, low-payoff approach to reemployment. The migrants were excluded from the analysis, since the sample was too small to estimate its complex behavior.

Finally, the Downriver program provides a useful example of the ways in which representatives of private industry and local elected officials can be involved in dislocated worker programs. Plant management and unions of affected plants have a valuable role to play in disseminating information about program services to dislocated workers. The Downriver experience suggests that worker participation is likely to be higher where plant management and unions work closely with the program by providing rosters of laid-off workers and sending outreach letters. Involving local employers in an oversight role, particularly with respect to design of training components, is a very effective strategy for enhancing their involvement in program design. Rather than involving employers in broad policy development or design issues, a more focused approach that assigns specific responsibilities makes the best use of employers. The Downriver program staff used a task force approach to involve employers that facilitated cross-agency linkages. The involvement of local elected officials is critical to the success of programs for dislocated workers. They need to be involved in the program from start-up, publicizing it in local communities and providing oversight support.

Program Effects on the Reemployment Experiences of Participants

This section summarizes the estimated effects of the Downriver program on the reemployment and earnings of participating workers. We first describe the outcome measures selected to characterize the reemployment process and the comparison strategy that we used. Because the policy conclusions drawn from this study depend in large degree on the soundness of both the outcome measures and the comparison groups, this section pays special attention to those aspects of the evaluation design. We offer descriptions of the data sources used in measurement of program impacts, and we discuss characteristics of the analysis sample. We then consider overall program effects on participants' employment and earnings and the differential impacts of training and job search.

Measurement of Outcome Variables. From a methodological standpoint, two major issues must be addressed in measuring the impact of any program. The first issue is the choice of outcome measures and the associated measurement period. The second and more critical is the choice of a comparison group. In the absence of a true experimental design, the methods used to adjust for differences between the treatment and comparison groups become critical. These issues are discussed in the next section.

As already noted, to assess the impact of the Downriver program, our analysis focused on three measures of labor market outcomes. The first measure, the reemployment rate, was defined as the percentage of workers in the sample who were ever reemployed during the period between layoff and the survey interview date. It is analogous to the placement rates used by employment and training program operators, but it is not the most appropriate summary indicator of performance.

The employment rate is more useful in capturing these additional dimensions. For each worker, the fraction of weeks employed during the period between layoff and interview was calculated. In addition to capturing the reemployment rate, the employment rate also summarizes the number of weeks it took reemployed workers to find a job and the stability of employment from that point to the interview. The average time between layoff and interview was approximately two-and-one-half years, so that the employment rate afforts a long-term indicator of program effect.

Finally, from a benefit-cost perspective, it is important to know the impact on the earnings of participating workers. Average weekly earnings, calculated as total earnings between layoff and interview divided by the total number of weeks in that period, is the most comprehensive of the three measures employed. Periods of unemployment were counted as zero earnings, so that the earnings measure is available for the entire sample.

Selection of a Comparison Group. The central problem in measuring the impacts of a program on participants is the choice of a comparison group. The comparison group provides an estimate of what would have happened to participants had there been no program. Program impacts, then, can be measured by comparing the actual outcomes observed for participants with the estimate provided by the comparison group.

Random assignment was not feasible in the Downriver program. Eligibility for program participation was offered on an entitlement basis to workers laid off from selected plants. Thus, the best choice for a comparison group was not obvious. This plant-based service strategy also posed the possibility that plant, as well as individual worker, characteristics could influence the reemployment process.

Several factors influenced the selection of comparison plants. Most important among them were the plant's previous layoff history and closure date and the income support benefits that its workers were eligible to receive. Whether the plant had experienced a prior layoff-recall pattern or had never had a major layoff prior to closure was expected to exert significant influence on workers' expectations about the probability of recall and hence on their level of program participation and job search effort. Further, a reasonably close matching of closure dates for program and comparison plants was necessary if we were to be sure that workers faced the same labor market conditions. Eligibility for different income support programs, including unemployment insurance, Supplemental Unemployment Benefits (SUB), or Trade Readjustment Assistance (TRA), was also important. Each benefit program offered a different compensation schedule and different duration of benefits. (During the study period, Michigan unemployment insurance regulations provided for a weekly benefit rate of 60 percent of the worker's average weekly wage, not to exceed the benefit maximum established for the applicable number of dependents. Benefits were payable for twenty-six weeks, with up to 13 weeks of extended benefits also payable to those exhasting their claims. TRA benefits were designed to provide up to 70 percent of the worker's average weekly wage for fifty-two weeks, with an additional twenty-six weeks of benefits provided if the worker enrolled in TRA-approved training.) Previous research has shown that both compensation level and duration of benefits exercise a significant influence over individuals' job search behavior. Finally, other factors involved in the selection process included plant size and type of products manufactured.

As already noted, the evaluation proceeded in two phases. Evalution of the second phase of the program was based only on experiences of the Ford Michigan Casting plant workers. The potential for confounding influences of unmeasured plant characteristics with program effects was most serious during this second phase.

The Ford and Chrysler assembly plants were similar with respect to many key characteristics. Both plants closed permanently in 1981, the Chrysler plant in July and the Ford plant in December. Both plants had experienced two major waves of layoffs, the first during the last quarter of 1979 and the first quarter of 1980 and the second during the third and fourth quarters of 1981. Workers from both plants were eligible for the same income maintenance benefits. Finally, the Ford plant was involved in fabrication rather than assembly, and a slightly different occupational skill mix was expected.

Adjusting for Differences Between Program-Eligible and Comparison Workers. Any nonrandomly generated comparison group will differ from program participants in both measured and unmeasured ways. Unmeasurable differences between participants and comparison groups pose the greater challenge in estimation of program impacts. It is reasonable to assume that participants and nonparticipants may differ in their expectations regarding the probability of recall and, more generally, in their desire for reemployment. To the extent that these expectations affect an individual's actual job search behavior, they will be correlated with reemployment success. If we compare participants with eligible nonparticipants and if our adjustment mechanisms do not fully capture the differences in expectations or motivation, we will confound motivation differences with the effects of program treatment. This is one example of a class of problems referred to as *selection bias*.

To avoid the confounding influence of selection bias, we estimated program effects by comparing the reemployment experiences of all program-eligible workers with the experiences of workers from plants that did not take part in the program. Participant self-selection was not a problem, because both groups contained individuals who were or, in the case of comparison plants, who would have been program participants. Both groups also included workers who did not participate or who would not have participated even if given the opportunity.

This comparison of program eligibles with workers from plants not in the program provides an estimate of the average effect on program-eligible workers. If we assume that the program had no effect on eligible workers who did not participate in the program, then the program effect on all eligible workers equals the program effect on participants times the participation rate. This relationship has a very simple interpretation: The impact of a program on the population eligible to receive its services is a function of the number of eligibles who decide to participate and of the average impact of the program on those participants. We can thus gauge the effect of the Downriver program on any participant outcome by dividing the estimated effect for eligible workers by the program participation rate. That is, if z represents the program effect and the subscripts p, np, and e the participants, nonparticipants, and eligibles respectively, then the program effect on eligible workers is a weighted average of the effect on participants and nonparticipants:

$$Z_e = Z_p \cdot P + Z_{np} \cdot (1 - P)$$

where P is the program participation rate. Assuming that there is no effect on nonparticipants, the program effect on participants is

$$Z_p = \frac{Z_e}{P}$$

The assumption of a zero program effect on nonparticipants is not innocuous, since it assumes that the demand for labor skills represented in the Downriver program is perfectly elastic. Since this is not true, there is displacement of other workers by Downriver eligibles that results in an overstatement of program impacts. A demonstration program could affect nonparticipants in another way: If participants monopolized existing subsidized employment and training services, they could displace persons who otherwise would have taken advantage of them. However, short-term class-size training programs of the Downriver program created additional training opportunities, so that it seems unlikely that the program affected subsidized opportunities for nonparticipants.

In estimating employment effects on the Downriver program, it was also necessary to control for variables that influenced reemployment experiences and that differed between the program-eligible and comparison groups. Variables thought to determine the reservation wage and the offer wage were considered especially important for the estimating models. Age, marital status, presence of children at home, and unemployment benefits replacement rate were included in the reemployment model as determinants of an individual's reservation wage. The first three factors were expected to affect the utility of forgone earnings; the fourth factor, the net size of those earnings. General work experience, years of formal education, tenure on the layoff job, and a dichotomous variable for being black were included as determinants of the potential wage offer. These are all key variables in a human capital explanation of earnings.

Besides these variables, the number of weeks between layoff and interview was included as an explanatory variable in the reemployment model, since reemployment rates after layoff are a function of time. The workers in our sample had been laid off at some point between the first quarter of 1979 and the end of 1981, and they were interviewed through the summer of 1983. This means that we had to control for the fact that workers were observed over different segments of time after layoff. (The wage rate on the layoff job was also a candidate for predicting an individual's potential wage offer. When included with the other variables in the reemployment model, its sign was postive as expected, but it was never statistically significant.) Finally, to control for changing economic conditions during the study period, we also included dummy variables for having been laid off in 1980 or 1981 in the models.

Given the differences in program operations and economic circumstances, all models were estimated separately for each phase. Further, as a control for unmeasured plant-specific effects within each model, effects were estimated with the inclusion of a dummy variable for each plant. In the models for the second phase, where there was only one eligible and one comparison plant, the coefficient on the eligible plant dummy is the estimated program effect. In the models for the first phase, the plant dummies provide an indication of whether there were unmeasured plant-specific effects. Because estimated effects differed with the comparison plants used, we have reported a range of estimated effects for the first-phase models. Finally, as a further check on the match between eligible and comparison plants, we also estimated employment and earnings models for the period between layoff and program start-up, a rough approximation of a preprogram period. There were no significant preprogram differences between eligible and comparison plants.

Data Sources and the Analysis Sample. From the program-eligible and comparison plants, a random sample of 2,750 laid-off workers was selected for interview. The sample was based on the employment rosters of study plants, with two exceptions. In all cases, because the study was to focus on reemployment after plant closure, workers who had been on disability or who had retired a year or more before the plant's closure were excluded from the sample frame. This was done to ensure that only individuals "at risk" of becoming reemployed were analyzed. In addition, for the Ford Michigan Casting and Chrysler assembly plants, salaried workers and workers with transfer or bumping rights were excluded. (A function of seniority, bumping rights entitled a worker to displace an individual at a lower grade level at another plant.) Finally, due to their small numbers, women were excluded from the sample.

Sampled workers from the first-phase plants were interviewed in the summer of 1982, and workers from the second-phase plants were interviewed in the spring of 1983. Given the timing of the layoffs in each instance, this interview strategy provided an observation period of approximately two-and-one-half years after layoff.

Workers still in the Detroit area (77 percent of the sample universe) were interviewed in person to collect information on their employment, training or education, and income sources and amounts between January 1, 1979 and the interview data. Migrants were excluded from the analysis, as noted earlier. Information on program treatment for workers who participated in the Downriver program was available from the program's management information system.

Overview of Employment and Earnings

Table 1 summarizes outcomes of the Downriver program on employment and earnings separately by phase and plant. The most striking finding is that, although at least two years had elapsed between the layoff and interview dates, an average of only 50 percent of the workers in the interview sample had ever found another job. This result is particularly striking given the demographic and labor market characteristics of the sample noted previously.

Since half the workers in our sample never found a job during the observation period, employment rates were also very low, averaging 20 percent. The third column of Table 1 displays average weekly earnings. Because of the low reemployment rates, sample members who earned an average of $469 per week on their layoff jobs earned an average of $69 per week during the period between layoff and interview.

Table 1. Characteristics of the Reemployment Process

	Reemployment rate[a]	Employment rate from layoff to interview[b]	Average weekly earnings from layoff to interview[c]
First-phase eligible workers:			
BASF ($N=152$)	72.8%	39.3%	$139
DANA ($N=236$)	53.1	25.4	95
First-phase comparison workers:			
Lear-Siegler ($N=200$)	54.5	22.0	61
Chrysler Foundry ($N=184$)	40.2	14.9	56
Second-phase program-eligible workers:			
Ford Motor Company Casting (MCC) ($N=594$)	48.9	20.6	65
Second-phase comparison workers:			
Chrysler Assembly ($N=341$)	41.4	16.2	37

[a] The reemployment rate is the percentage of workers ever employed between layoff and interview.

[b] The employment rate equals weeks worked between layoff and interview (including zero for workers never reemployed) divided by the number of weeks in the period times 100.

[c] Average weekly earnings equal total earnings between layoff and interview (including zero for workers never reemployed) divided by the number of weeks in the period.

Effects on Employment and Earnings for the First Phase of the Program. Table 2 presents program effects on employment and earnings for DANA and BASF workers who were eligible for the first phase of the Downriver program services. There were relatively large impacts on reemployment and earnings of participating workers; however, the impacts for BASF workers were more pronounced and robust than the effects for DANA employees.

Considering employment effects first, Table 2 shows that the Downriver program increased both the reemployment rates and employment rates of program-eligible BASF workers by approximately 11 percent. These estimated effects are not sensitive to the plants included in the comparison sample. This robustness increases our confidence in the observed impacts for the BASF group, particularly in light of our concerns about unmeasured plant-specific effects.

Table 2. Program Effects on Reemployment, First Phase

	Comparison group	
	Lear-Siegler only	Lear-Siegler and Chrysler Foundry
Effect on reemployment rate		
BASF: all program eligibles[a]	12.3%**	9.8**
program participants	21.4**	17.0**
DANA: all programs eligibles	8.1*	3.8*
program participants	18.8*	8.7*
Effect on employment rate from layoff to interview		
BASF: all program eligibles	11.6**	10.6**
program participants	20.1**	18.4**
DANA: all program eligibles	3.5*	2.5*
program participants	6.1*	5.8*
Effect on average weekly earnings from layoff to interview		
BASF: all program eligibles	$ 63.9**	25.6**
program participants	110.9**	44.4**
DANA: all program eligibles	52.6*	14.3*
program participants	121.8*	33.1*

Note: Models of the reemployment rate, employment rate, and average weekly earnings were estimated with dummy variables for the BASF, DANA, and Chrysler Foundry plants, along with worker characteristics, as right-hand side variables. Estimated coefficients and t-statistics are not reported in this volume. A set of appendix tables for this study may be obtained through the editor of this sourcebook. Program effects are estimated by comparing our estimated coefficients on the plant dummy variables as described in the text. Asterisks indicate that the program effect is statistically significant at the 5 percent (**) or the 10 percent (*) level (two-tailed test).

[a] Effects on participants equal the program effect on eligible workers divided by the program participation rate for each plant's workers. For BASF, this rate was 57.6 percent; for DANA, 43.2 percent.

Viewed in the context of the actual reemployment and employment rates presented in Table 1, we note that the Downriver program increased BASF workers' reemployment rates from an estimated 62 percent without the program to 73 percent—a relative increase of 18 percent. In addition, the program improved BASF workers' overall employment experiences since layoff, increasing employment rates during that period from 28 percent to 39 percent. Finally, because these estimated effects are for all BASF program eligibles, they are necessarily lower than the effects expected for participants. If we divide the estimates by the participation rate for BASF workers, we see that the Downriver program increased their employment by approximately 20 percentage points—a sizable impact by most standards.

Program effects on earnings for BASF workers follow a similar pattern. Using only Lear-Siegler as a comparison plant, the Downriver program was estimated to increase average weekly earnings after layoff by $64 over the amount that could be expected if there had been no program. This translates into approximately $3,300 per year. The size of the estimated earnings effect is sensitive to the composition of the comparison sample: When Chrysler Foundry workers are included, the effect is reduced to $25 per week per eligible worker. In part, this reflects the fact that Chrysler workers were the highest paid and BASF workers were the lowest paid prior to layoff. Given the size, significance, and overall robustness of the estimated impacts, we conclude that the Downriver program was effective in increasing employment and earnings for BASF workers after layoff.

Table 2 shows a slightly different story for DANA workers. Considering all three outcome measures, note that the program did yield positive impacts, but in no instance were these effects as large or as strong as those for the BASF group. In addition, Table 2 reveals that estimated impacts for DANA workers were much more sensitive to the composition of the comparison group. Examining employment after layoff first, we note that the program increased eligible DANA workers' reemployment rates by 8 percentage points and their overall employment rates by about half that amount when they were compared with Lear-Siegler workers. These effects are smaller than those observed for BASF workers, and they are sensitive to the comparison group used. When the Chrysler Foundry plant is included, the effect on the reemployment rate drops to 4 percentage points, and the effect on the employment rate, to 3 percent. Finally, in contrast to effects for the BASF group, effects for the DANA group are statistically significant at only the 20 percent level.

As is the case for BASF workers, effects for participants are somewhat larger than for all eligibles. Dividing the estimated effects by the participation rate for DANA workers (43.2 percent), we see that these effects roughly double in size. Indeed, the lower participation rate of DANA workers (43.2 percent compared with 57.6 percent for BASF workers) contributes in large part to the smaller effects observed here.

Despite the smaller effects exerted by the Downriver program on

DANA workers' employment experiences, the program did produce significant impacts on average weekly earnings after layoff. As with BASF workers, these estimated effects ranged from $14 to $53 per week per eligible worker depending on the comparison group used. Again, effects were significant at the 10 percent level, yet in comparison with employment effects they were disproportionately large. This suggests that, for DANA workers, earnings effects may have resulted from reemployment at higher-wage jobs rather than from more rapid or more stable reemployment.

Table 3 provides additional support for this analysis by considering impacts of the Downriver program on participants' wages, weekly hours, and earnings after layoff. Here, effects are estimated only for reemployed indi-

Table 3: Program Effects on Wages, Hours, and Earnings After Layoff for Reemployed Participants, First Phase

	Comparison Group	
Program plant	Lear-Siegler only	Lear-Siegler and Chrysler Foundry (90% confidence interval)[a]
Effect on average hourly wage rate[b]		
BASF	2.46**	2.52** (1.65 — 3.37)
DANA	0.64	0.22 (−.64 — 1.08)
Effect on average weekly hours[b]		
BASF	4.7	5.4 (1.8 — 9.1)
DANA	−1.6	0.1 (−3.9 — 4.1)
Effect on average weekly earnings[b]		
BASF	134.00**	132.46** (92 — 172)
DANA	8.81	20.44 (−20 — 60)

Note: The results are only for reemployed participants.

[a] Regression models were used to estimate program effects on reemployed eligible workers. Program effects on participants are the program effects for eligibles divided by the proportion of reemployed eligibles who were program participants. For DANA eligibles, this fraction is .49. For BASF eligibles, this fraction is .65. Asterisks indicate that the program effect is statistically significant at the 5 percent (**) or 10 percent (*) level (two-tailed test).

[b] Outcomes are calculated from a weighted average of hourly wages, weekly hours, or weekly earnings on jobs after layoff through the interview date with the weights equal to the proportion of employed time spent at each job.

viduals rather than for all eligible workers regardless of their employment status. To measure program effects for participants, program effects on eligible workers were then divided by the proportion of participants among the reemployed eligibles.

Recall that restricting the sample to reemployed workers may bias the program effects estimated in Table 3. It was reasonable to argue that unmeasured factors, such as motivation or aptitude, were similar on average for the eligible and comparison groups as a whole. Yet, this may not be true for the eligible and comparison workers who became reemployed. (These unmeasured factors must be correlated with the probability of reemployment; if they are not, there is no problem with differences between eligible and comparison groups. Given this correlation, the fact that the proportion of eligible workers reemployed was higher than the proportion of comparison workers implies that the mean level of these unmeasured factors will differ for reemployed eligible and comparison workers.) In the case examined here, the coefficient on the program-eligible variable in our regression models measured both the effect of the Downriver program and the effects of differences in unmeasured characteristics that are related to employment. Thus, the effects described in this section must be interpreted with caution.

Turning first to the hourly wage results, we note that wages were between $1.00 and $2.50 higher for reemployed participants in the Downriver program than for comparison workers, depending on the plant and the composition of the comparison sample. Again, effects are larger, stronger, and more robust for the BASF group. The program showed no effects on weekly hours of work; participants were employed on average at jobs with a standard work week and few overtime hours. Finally, the wage and hours effects combine to produce a substantial program effect on average weekly earnings while employed. Again, this effect was largest for BASF workers—more than $130 per week. Effects for DANA participants were much lower but still significant.

Table 3 thus suggests that our hypothesis about the source of effects for DANA workers may not be correct: Wages for reemployed DANA participants were not significantly higher than wages for their counterparts in each comparison group. At the same time, given our cautions about interpretation of effects estimated only for reemployed individuals, we reiterate that the program effects presented in Table 3 reflect both program effects and unmeasured differences between groups that are also related to the probability of reemployment. Thus, we must conclude that the program effects observed for both BASF and DANA workers stem from a combination of effects on reemployment probability, employment stability, reemployment wage rates, and the fraction of eligibles who participated in the Downriver program.

What can we conclude from this review of impacts of the first phase of the Downriver program? Although estimated effects differ in size, strength, and robustness, the program did yield significant impacts on employment and earnings for participating BASF and DANA workers. Effects were most pronounced for BASF workers: a 20 percentage point increase in participants' reemployment rates and employment after layoff and a $77 per week increase in earnings over what would be expected if there were no program. Most important, these estimated effects were similar regardless of the composition of the comparison sample.

In contrast, effects for DANA workers were smaller and less robust: an average 13 percentage point effect on reemployment probability, a 6 percentage point effect on employment rates, and a $75 per week increase in earnings after layoff. However, even these smaller average effects reflected fairly important differences depending on the comparison sample used. We further conclude that, while the Downriver program produced effects for both BASF and DANA workers, differences between workers from these plants conditioned the magnitude of the effects in ways that our models did not capture.

Effects on Employment and Earnings for the Second Phase of the Program. Table 4 shows the estimated effects of the Downriver program on reemployment and earnings for the Ford workers who were made eligible for the second phase of the program. In contrast to the sizable and significant effects observed for BASF and DANA workers, Table 4 shows negative, yet for the most part insignificant, effects for the Ford workers.

Table 4. Program Effects on Reemployment, Second Phase

	Comparison group	
Program plant	Chrysler Assembly only	Chrysler Assembly and Chrysler Foundry
Effect on reemployment rate		
Ford MCC: all program eligibles	-16.4**	- 8.2**
program participants[a]	-38.4**	-19.2*
Effect of employment rate from layoff to interview:		
Ford MCC: all program eligibles	- 4.0	- 2.4
program participants	- 9.4	- 5.6
Effect on average weekly earnings from layoff to interview:		
Ford MCC: all program eligibles	- 1	- 8
program participants	- 2.3	-18.9

Note: Models of the reemployment rate, employment rate, and average weekly earnings were estimated with dummy variables for the Ford MCC and Chrysler Foundry plants, along with worker characteristics, as right-hand variables. Program effects are estimated by comparing the coefficients on the plant dummy variables as described in the text. Asterisks indicate that the program effect is statistically significant at the 5 percent (**) or the 10 percent (*) level (two-tailed test).

[a] Effects on participants equal the program effect on eligibles divided by the participant rate, 42.6 percent.

Compared to workers for both the Chrysler Assembly and Chrysler Foundry plants, Ford workers experienced significantly lower reemployment rates after layoff. When the comparison is made with the Chrysler Assembly plant, this difference is estimated at 16 percentage points. Including the Chrysler Foundry plant in the comparison group reduced the differential by half, but it does not change our conclusion: The second phase of the Downriver program did not increase the reemployment rates of Ford workers. In fact, our analysis suggests that the program may actually have depressed reemployment rates; some possible explanations for this are discussed later.

Turning to effects on employment rates and earnings after layoff, we see virtually no difference between Ford workers and those in the comparison group. In all cases, Ford workers are predicted to be worse off than workers from the Chrysler plants, but estimated effects are neither large nor significant. Overall employment rates for eligible Ford workers are predicted to be 4 percentage points lower as a result of the program, and weekly earnings after layoff are predicted to be between one and eight dollars lower depending on the composition of the comparison sample. As noted in Table 4, estimated effects on participants are necessarily larger but not significant.

Table 5 supports this pattern of no effects. Here, program effects on wages, weekly working hours, and earnings after layoff are shown for reemployed Ford workers. Bearing in mind our cautions regarding the interpretattion of results for reemployed participants—that is, the effects shown here

Table 5: Program Effects on Wages, Hours, and Earnings After Layoff for Reemployed Participants, Second Phase

Program plant	Comparison Group	
	Chrysler Assembly only	Chrysler Assembly and Chrysler Foundry (90% confidence interval)
Effects on average hourly rate		
Ford MCC	9.95	−0.19 (−1.1 — .72)
Effect on average weekly hours		
Ford MCC	1.0	− .91 (−5.4 — 3.6)
Effect on average weekly earnings		
Ford MCC	36.34	8.25 (−38.5 — 55.0)

Note: Regression models were used to estimate program effects on reemployed eligible workers. Program effects on participants are the program effect on eligibles divided by the proportion of reemployed eligibles who were program participants (.395). Asterisks indicate that the program effect is statistically significant at the 5 percent (**) or 10 percent (*) level (two-tailed test).

reflect both the effects of the Downriver program and the effects of other, unmeasured characteristics correlated with reemployment—Table 5 shows no significant effects for any of the three outcome measures. Moreover, we note that the 90 percent confidence interval around the reported estimates obtained when we included both Chrysler plants in the comparison group includes both positive and negative values. This creates a great deal of uncertainty about the magnitude of these effects.

To summarize these findings, our analysis shows that the first phase of the Downriver program resulted in increased employment and earnings for both former BASF and DANA workers but that the second phase of the program showed no such effects for Ford workers. In fact, our analysis suggests that the program may have actually reduced Ford workers' reemployment prospects during the observation period. This could have happened if the program made Ford workers more selective in accepting employment or if they were enrolled in program training for a disproportionate share of the observation period. However, the data on service use and program participation suggest that training enrollment is an unlikely explanation.

Interpreting Differences in Estimated Impacts: Some Likely Explanations and Their Implications

How can we explain these rather different results? More important, how confident can we be that they are real, and what are their implications for generalization?

Several factors may explain the differences in impact across the first and second phases of the program. First, we could surmise that the program treatment had changed in some way between phases and that the services offered in the second phase were simply not effective. Yet, there was basically no change in the types of services delivered. From an administrative perspective, the Downriver program was more tightly structured during its second phase. So, we discount program changes as a source of the negative effects in the second phase.

Another explanation might be that the characteristics of eligible workers changed between phases and that the Downriver program was simply not effective for the second group as a result of the differences. Here, the evidence is mixed. BASF workers were more likely to participate than DANA or Ford workers were, but participation rates for all three eligible plants were high. Moreover, workers from the three plants were very similar except for age distribution, wages before layoff, and income support benefits.

An examination of the estimated coefficients for the employment and earnings models shows that, if there are differences between the first- and second-phase eligibles, our measured variables do not reflect them. For most variables included in the models, the coefficients are estimated precisely, they are of similar magnitude, and they show the signs found in previous reduced-form models of the job search process. The only exceptions are the race variable and the variable measuring income support benefits.

The income support variable deserves further discussion. For the first-phase DANA and BASF workers, a 10 percentage point increase in the unemployment benefits replacement rate was estimated to have reduced the reemployment rate by approximately 4 percentage points. For Ford workers, the corresponding reduction was lower; an estimated 2 percentage points. This suggests that first-phase workers were slightly more sensitive to the level and duration of the income support that they received than second-phase workers were. Recalling that the Ford workers were receiving generous TRA payments, which could in theory continue for up to one-and-one-half years, the lower elasticity makes sense. Thus, while for the most part the first- and second-phase Downriver eligibles were similar, we do see evidence that second-phase eligibles behaved slightly differently.

Finally, there may be some unmeasured differences between the first- and second-phase workers. In particular, program enrollment was longer for the Ford workers (more than one year, compared with about eight months for the DANA and BASF workers), and training completion rates were lower. Combining this information with anecdotal evidence of absenteeism and drug abuse among this plant's work force suggests that there may have been important motivational differences between the Ford workers and their counterparts at DANA and BASF.

A third explanation for the poor performance of the program in its second phase was the worsening local labor market situation. Unemployment rates for the Detroit labor market averaged 13.1 percent in 1980 and 1981, but they rose to 15.7 percent during 1982 and to 17 percent in 1983. It may be possible that no assistance program can yield large employment effects under such conditions. This could be particularly true if the effects of the Downriver program are primarily improvement of participants' positions in the employment queue rather than enhancement of their human capital—if the queue is very long, and if few of those waiting for jobs are hired, movement from the third quartile to the first in employability may not result in a job. At the same time, because such economic conditions are presented as an optimal situation for undertaking training—because there are few jobs, the opportunity costs associated with leaving the labor force for retraining are low—we might expect to see earnings effects attributable to the Downriver program over the longer term.

A related explanation is that it took individuals much longer to become reemployed during the second phase. If our observation period was not long enough, we might well have missed seeing both employment and earnings effects for Ford workers. Although our observation period (the time between layoff and the interview data) was approximately two-and-one-half years on average, when we consider, first, that workers waited an average of thirteen to twenty-six weeks after layoff before enrolling in the program and, second, that second-phase participants were enrolled for an average of more than a year, we may actually be viewing very little postparticipation time for the Ford workers.

We examined the quarterly pattern of reemployment experiences for program-eligible and comparison workers separately by program phase. For each quarter, we computed the number of workers at risk of being unemployed and divided that into the number of workers finding employment during the period. The result is an estimate of the probability of reemployment in that period for a person who has not yet found employment. If we call this estimate h_t, then the reemployment rate through period T is expressed as

$$1 - \prod_{t-1}^{T} (1 - h_t)^t$$

What we found confirmed what we presented in Table 2 and Table 4: Reemployment rates were much higher for BASF and DANA program-eligible workers. In addition, the differences in reemployment rates over time between program-eligible and comparison workers were greater for the first-phase group. In comparison, the second-phase Ford workers were reemployed much more slowly: One year after layoff, only 29 percent had become reemployed, compared with 45 percent of their counterparts at BASF and DANA. Two years after layoff, the differential still stood at 14 percent.

Given this review of possible explanations for the effects we observed, the most likely explanation appears to be that there are unmeasured plant-specific differences, which the variables included in our estimating models have not completely captured. This explanation is supported both by slight differences in impacts for BASF and DANA workers and by the sensitivity of some of the estimated impacts to the composition of the comparison group.

This explanation has two implications. First, differences between the program service plants are likely to exert an impact on workers' reemployment irrespective of the Downriver program treatment. Including more plants in the program service group, particularly during the second phase of the program, would have substantially lessened the risk of confounding unmeasured plant differences with program effects. Because only one plant was included in the second-phase evaluation, we must necessarily place more confidence in the results of the first phase of the program. At the same time, that the program made services available to only a few selected plants reduces our ability to generalize from these results.

The second implication can be stated as a question: How does this explanation affect the internal validity of our results? What do these unmeasured plant differences portend for our comparison strategy? Indeed, the sensitivity of some of our estimates to the composition of the comparison group suggests that our plant matching may not have been as successful as we would have liked. As a partial test of this problem, all employment and earnings models were estimated for the period between layoff and program start-up.

If there were differences between program-eligible and comparison workers, then those differences should be reflected in this preprogram period; however, no such differences emerged. This suggests that, on balance, the comparison strategy was effective and that the findings are internally valid. At the same time, a true randomized experiment would have been preferable.

Effects of the Downriver Program by Type of Program Service

For several reasons, it is important to estimate the incremental effects of training, over and above the effects of job search, on participants' employment and earnings. First, training has historically and reflexively been prescribed as a remedy for structural unemployment. Concerns about changes in the organization of production brought about by automation and technological advances have recently served to focus attention on efforts to retrain and retool our work force. Yet, the effectiveness of training in increasing employment has been shown to vary widely, depending on the type of training offered, the characteristics of trainees, and the structure and management of the training program.

Second, training is considerably more expensive to provide than job search assistance. In the Downriver program, average training costs per trainee were more than twice the average costs of job search assistance. The time frame for measurement of the benefits due to training is important for this last point. Because Downriver staff focused on developing training opportunities for entry-level positions in growth occupations, it is highly unlikely that we will see significant earnings gains in the period immediately after training.

Table 6 displays the time pattern of reemployment rates separately by program phase. We show reemployment rates by number of months for program enrollment for participants enrolled in training and for participants receiving only job search assistance. The framework for computation of these effects is the same as that used in computing employment rates after layoff.

For participants in the first phase of the program, reemployment rates for those enrolled in training were lower than the rates observed for those receiving only job search assistance during the first six months of participation. This finding is roughly consistent with the average duration of the first-phase training program, eight months. After this period, reemployment rates for training became higher, ending with a 9 percentage point difference in the twelfth month after enrollment. These differences are only suggestive, since the small sample sizes produce standard errors too large to support statistically significant conclusions.

For participants in the second phase of the program, we see no such crossover effect in reemployment rates. The difference between trainees and those receiving job search assistance is consistently large and negative. The most likely explanation is the high training dropout rate observed for Ford

Table 6. Reemployment Rates by Months from Program Enrollment

Months from program enrollment	Phase I Participants enrolled in classroom training	Phase I Participants enrolled in job search only	Phase I Difference in reemployment rates	Phase II Participants enrolled in classroom training	Phase II Participants enrolled in job search only	Phase II Difference in reemployment rates
1	4.5 (2.5)	6.1 (2.9)	1.6	0.8 (0.8)	7.4 (2.4)	6.6
2	7.5 (3.2)	12.1 (3.9)	4.6	2.6 (1.4)	12.0 (3.0)	9.4
3	13.4 (4.0)	19.7 (4.7)	6.3	4.3 (1.9)	13.9 (3.3)	9.6
4	20.9 (4.7)	24.2 (5.1)	3.3	6.0 (1.9)	15.7 (3.5)	9.7
5	31.3 (5.3)	28.8 (5.4)	2.5	7.8 (2.5)	18.5 (3.7)	10.7
6	32.8 (5.7)	33.3 (5.6)	−0.5	9.5 (2.7)	22.2 (3.9)	−12.7
7	40.3 (5.6)	37.9 (5.8)	2.4	13.7 (3.1)	24.0 (4.0)	−10.3
8	49.3 (5.6)	42.4 (5.9)	6.9	16.2 (3.3)	25.9 (4.2)	− 9.7
9	52.2 (5.9)	47.0 (5.9)	5.2	19.6 (3.6)	27.8 (4.2)	− 8.2
10	53.6 (5.8)	48.5 (6.1)	5.1	20.4 (3.7)	32.4 (4.4)	−12.0
11	56.5 (5.7)	50.0 (6.1)	6.5	21.2 (3.7)	36.1 (4.5)	−15.7
12	59.3 (5.6)	50.0 (6.2)	9.3	23.8 (3.8)	37.9 (4.6)	−14.1
Sample size	67	66		115	108	

Note: The sample includes program participants enrolled in job search only or in classroom training who were not reemployed before program enrollment. To adjust for censoring imposed by the observation period, reemployment rates are estimated from the period-by-period conditional probabilities of reemployment in a life table framework. Standard errors of the reemployment rate are in parentheses.

participants. Because our training variable captures enrollment rather than completion, those who start a training program and then drop out to look for work are included in the training group.

Moreover, these results have not been adjusted for the confounding effects of differences in average characteristics between participants receiving training and participants receiving only job search assistance. It is likely that the two groups differed, because the operators of the Downriver program used relatively well-defined guidelines to select participants for training.

For participants in the second phase of the program, the aptitude test scores used to assign participants to classroom training or job search were available. Because we have no reason to believe that the test scores necessarily correlated with reemployment, we used them to predict training enrollment. This predicted probability was then included in models estimating the impact of program training on reemployment rates. Results are shown in Table 7.

The first row of Table 7 shows the unadjusted difference between re-

Table 7. Incremental Effect of Training on Reemployment Rates of Participants

	Difference between reemployment rates for participants receiving both training and job search assistance and participants receiving only job search assistance (90 percent confidence interval)
Unadjusted[a]	−14.1
Adjusted for worker characteristics[b]	
Ordinary least-squares estimate	−14.5
	(−24.5, −4.4)
Instrumental variables estimate[c]	17.0
	(−24.6, 58.6)
Adjusted for worker characteristics and potential job search weeks[d]	
Ordinary least-squares estimate	5.2
	(−10.3, 20.7)
Instrumental variables estimate	12.2
	(−41.9, 66.3)

[a] The unadjusted difference equals reemployment rate of participants enrolled in training minus reemployment rate of participants receiving only job search assistance.

[b] Controls for worker characteristics are provided by estimating a coefficient on a dummy variable for training enrollment in a regression of reemployment on that variable and worker characteristics.

[c] Instrumental variables estimates attempt to adjust for the bias in estimated training effects caused by the nonrandom process used to select participants for training.

[d] Potential job search weeks equal weeks between the end of training and the interview for trainees and weeks between program enrollment and the interview for participants receiving only job search assistance.

employment rates for trainees and nontrainees. This difference is simply the 14 percentage point disadvantage reported in Table 6. The second panel of Table 7 adjusts this estimated differential, first, for differences in worker characteristics and, second, for differences proxied by aptitude and achievement test scores. We see that adjusting for measurable worker characteristics does little to change the estimated differential impact — it is still large and negative — but that adjusting for unmeasured differences captured by achievement test scores reverses the sign effect. This reversal suggests that training was indeed reserved for individuals with poor labor market opportunities. Staff had maintained that workers with immediately marketable skills would be offered only job search assistance, while those who lacked marketable skills yet who had the aptitude to succeed at training would be placed in classroom and on-the-job positions. The results presented in Table 7 corroborate this assignment policy: Once these aptitude factors are controlled for, program training is estimated to have had a positive impact on participants' reemployment. However, because sample sizes were small, the effects were not statistically significant.

The third panel of Table 7 employs an additional adjustment, the number of weeks after training that an individual was available for job search. For trainees, this period was measured as time elapsed between training exit and interview date; for nontrainees, as the time between program enrollment and interview data. As mentioned before, it is important that we observe trainees long enough to see the results of job search after training. We do not want to compare outcomes for trainees and nontrainees while trainees are still enrolled. At the same time, because training programs are of different lengths and especially because length of enrollment varied considerably during the second phase due to high dropout rates, we have adjusted for potential search weeks in our third set of estimates. Table 7 further shows that training effects are positive, though still not significant, when we control for search weeks. Thus, we must conclude that, despite adjustment for unobserved characteristics and time spent out of the labor force due to training enrollment, Downriver program training did not significantly improve participants' reemployment experiences.

This finding does not necessarily imply that training does not help workers served by the program to become reemployed. First and most important, the size and signs of the estimated marginal effects suggest that they may have been effective, but the small sample sizes prevent us from stating this with confidence. Second, while we believe that our instrumental variables capture the training assignment process, our estimated effects could be biased, with the direction of the bias unknown, if the achievement test scores were in fact correlated with employment outcomes.

Summary and Conclusions

The study described in this chapter has presented evidence that the first phase of the Downriver dislocated worker program had significant but mixed effects on the employment and earnings of participating workers. There were large effects for BASF workers. The estimated effects are robust regardless of the plants included in the comparison sample. The effects for former DANA employees were small and less robust but still significant. However, the magnitude of the effects changes slightly when the composition of the comparison sample is varied.

The large effects observed for the BASF and DANA workers in the first phase of the Downriver program were not observed for Ford workers in the second phase. In fact, the program actually decreased reemployment rates and had no effect on overall employment rates and earnings. Given the large positive effects observed for the first phase of operations and the more structured approach taken toward service delivery during the second phase of the program, we might expect similar results from the second phase of operations. How do we explain and then interpret the divergent results?

One explanation involves the worsening economy in the Downriver area between 1981 and 1983, the second phase of the program. Another explanation is that poor labor market conditions make it more difficult for participants to find jobs during periods of high unemployment, and the jobs that they find are inherently more unstable.

However, the most compelling explanation for the differences in impact observed is unmeasured differences between plants in both the program-eligible and comparison groups. The variation in the size of estimated effects across the three program-eligible plants, plus the sensitivity of these effects to the composition of the comparison group, suggests that unmeasured differences were at work.

If these differences exist, two concerns must be raised. The first relates to the internal validity of our estimates: How confident can we be that we can make causal inferences regarding the source of our estimated effects? The second relates to external validity: our ability to generalize these results to other situations.

With regard to the issue of internal validity, we are comfortable with the comparison plants chosen; in particular, we can find no preprogram employment or earnings differentials between eligible and comparison plant workers. We feel most confident in the case of BASF workers, where effects are large, significant, and stable regardless of the comparison plants used. In addition, we are confident that the effects for DANA workers were significant, but the sensitivity of estimates to the composition of the comparison group gives rise to questions about their actual magnitude. Finally, we also are confident that there are no positive program effects for Ford workers served during the second program phase.

We have greater concerns about the issue of the external validity of these results. First, it is dangerous to extrapolate the Downriver findings to areas with substantially different economies. Second, it is even more dangerous to generalize about the overall effects of the program from the three plants included in the service population. The small number of plants included in the evaluation makes it equally dangerous to extrapolate findings to any other population. We are especially cautious about such generalizations for the second phase, where only one of the two service plants could be included in the evaluation. Including still more plants in both the program-eligible and the comparison group would have further improved our confidence in the generalizability of results to other, similar locations.

Last, our findings suggest that the Downriver program significantly increased the access of participants to training opportunities but that this training did not result in significant improvements in employment prospects. However, we cannot conclude that program training produced no beneficial effects, principally because of the small sample sizes. Given the cost of training as a remedy for structural employment, our analysis suggests that a more rigorous test involving random assignment to training or job search services would yield extremely important policy information.

Jane Kulik is manager of the labor economics research area for Abt Associates, Inc., Arlington, Massachusetts.

D. Alton Smith is visiting professor, United States Military Academy, Lexington, Massachusetts.

Ernst W. Stromsdorfer is professor and chair of the economics department, Washington State University, Pullman.

Can alternative ways of administering and guaranteeing the flow of child support payments enhance the welfare of children of separated or divorced parents?

A Design for an Economic Analysis: The Wisconsin Child Support Demonstration

Irwin Garfinkel
Thomas Corbett

In the summer of 1980, a research team from the Institute for Research on Poverty (IRP) contracted with the Wisconsin Department of Health and Social Services (DHSS) to examine the existing Wisconsin child support system in order to design and evaluate alternatives to it. In February 1982, the IRP delivered a three-volume report entitled *Child Support: Weaknesses of the Old and Features of a Proposed New System* (Garfinkel and Melli, 1982). As the title suggests, the report recommended that Wisconsin adopt a new child support system. The first step in that direction was to demonstrate the new system in

> The experiment for which an evaluation is proposed in this chapter was partially implemented as of June 1985. In the first half of 1984, ten Wisconsin counties began wage withholding for child support payment collection, and ten control counties were identified. In addition, a percentage-of-income support standard was recommended, but not required, by state authorities. Observations regarding this latter dimension will depend on the natural variation that occurs as awards are made. A third component of the proposed experiment, the minimum benefit, will be implemented in January 1987. The authors are proceeding with evaluations described here, as applicable, and have not yet published results.

several Wisconsin counties. This chapter describes a design for the demonstration and for its evaluation.

The first four sections discuss the major findings of the February 1982 report. These sections highlight the weaknesses of the current child support system, the goals and constraints underlying the new program, the major features of the new system, and the estimated savings of the new system. The next eight sections focus on the proposed demonstration. These sections discuss what will be demonstrated, what we want to learn from the demonstration, the data required and the data sources available, the evaluation design, how long the demonstration should last, whether the demonstration should be limited to new cases, the nature and size of the samples, and the design of the statistical analysis.

Weaknesses of the Current Child Support System

The U.S. child support system fosters parental irresponsibility. It is inequitable, and it therefore exacerbates tensions between former spouses. Finally, it impoverishes children. Although experiences in Wisconsin are demonstrably better than average, the same criticisms apply there — only with less force.

National statistics contain the evidence of parental irresponsibility (U.S. Department of Commerce, 1981). Only 59 percent of the women eligible for support have received child support awards. Of those awarded child support, only 49 percent received the full amount due them, and 29 percent received nothing. Child support is collected from only 10 percent of the absent fathers of AFDC children. In Wisconsin, it is collected from 15 percent.

The child support system is inequitable because the amount of support that an absent parent pays depends not just on ability to pay but on the varying attitudes of local judges, district attorneys, and welfare officials; the beliefs and attitudes of both parents; the current relationship between the parents; and the skills of their respective lawyers (Yee, 1979). Almost every absent parent can find someone earning more who pays less. Nearly every custodial parent knows someone who is receiving more though the child's father earns less. Because of this and the absence of firm, determinative legislative guidelines, child support is a major source of continuing tension between many former spouses. Perhaps the most inequitable aspect of the current system is the capriciousness with which it is enforced. More absent fathers than not pay no child support. Most who do not pay suffer no consequences. Yet, others, albeit a small percentage, are thrown into jail (Chambers, 1979).

Finally, the widespread failure of the system to ensure that absent parents pay child support impoverishes their children and shifts the burden of financial support to the public sector. Nearly half of all children living in households headed by women are poor and on welfare (Danziger, 1981). Welfare — which was designed to aid those not expected to work — is no longer the best way of providing aid to children with single mothers, because we now

Table 1. Estimated Benefits and Costs of Alternative Child Support Reform Plans for Fiscal 1980 in Wisconsin

Description of Plan		Tax Rate Percentage	Millions of Dollars					Percentage Who Pay At Least the Minimum	
	Benefit		(1) Benefits	(2) Tax on Absent Parent	(3) Tax on Custodial Parent	(4) AFDC Savings	(5) Net Savings	(6) Absent Parent	(7) Absent Parent Plus Custodial Parent
First Child	$3,500	20	$590	$419	$83	$169	$81	40%	57%
Second Child	1,500	10							
Maximum		40							
First Child	3,500	15	547	340	81	165	39	30	44
Second Child	1,500	10							
Maximum		40							
First Child	2,000	20	461	393	46	146	125	60	77
Second Child	1,000	10							
Maximum		40							
First Child	2,000	15	397	314	48	122	87	51	68

Source: 1975 state survey of income and education and authors' estimates.

expect single mothers to work. In view of the fact that one in every two children born today will spend some time in a single-parent family before reaching age eighteen (Moynihan, 1981), the inadequacy of our child support system constitutes a major social problem.

Goals and Constraints for a New Child Support System

The proposed reform has four goals: to establish and collect child support equitably and efficiently, to assure a minimal level of support to children with a living absent parent, to improve the economic opportunities available to single-parent families, and to reduce the number of single-parent families on welfare. There are three major constraints: to avoid increasing costs to general taxpayers, to guard against overtaxing absent parents, and to prevent any reduction in the well-being of AFDC recipients.

Recommendations for a New System

Our analysis suggests that these goals and constraints would best be met by enacting legislation that created a new system for establishing, collecting, and distributing child support paymnts. The most equitable method of establishing child support obligations is to legislate a simple normative formula for child support. The most effective way of collecting support from absent parents is to assess it as a tax and collect it through a wage-withholding system. The best way of guaranteeing a minimum level of support to all children with a living absent parent and of reducing the dependence of such children on welfare is to pay benefits to all eligible children, rich and poor alike. In short, under the child support program proposed here, all absent parents are required to share their income with their children. All children who have an absent parent are entitled to the child support paid by their absent parent or to a publicly guaranteed minimum, whichever is larger. In cases where the absent parent cannot pay child support equal to the minimum, a supplement would be provided out of general revenues that would otherwise be spent on welfare. Finally, in order both to avoid public subsidies to families who are not in need and to reduce budget costs, the custodial parent would be subject to a special surtax up to the amount of the public subsidy in cases where the absent parent pays less than the minimum.

We make no recommendations on the level of tax rates on absent parents or minimum child support benefits. Instead, in Table 1 we report the effects on public savings or the cost of adopting alternative tax rates and minimum benefit levels. Ultimately, the fundamental decisions about tax rate and benefit levels will emerge from the political process.

Savings of a New System

Crude cost estimates suggest that the proposed new child support program could result in modest to substantial savings. The estimates are crude for several reasons. First, the data used are for 1975. Substantial changes have since occurred in the eligible population. Second, because there are no direct data on the incomes of absent parents, we had to rely on the characteristics of custodial parents to estimate this crucial piece of information. Third, in the absence of experience with the effectiveness of the new collection system, we could only guess how much more efficient the new system would be. Despite these and other shortcomings, we believe that the cost estimates in Table 1 give us the right order of magnitude. Table 1 presents estimates for four different proposals; administrative costs are ignored. In all cases, it is assumed that 100 percent of the potential tax revenue from the absent parent is collected.

In the first two plans, minimum benefits are equal to $3,500 for the first child and $1,500 for each subsequent child. In the third and fourth plans, minimum benefits are equal to $2,000 for the first child and $1,000 for each subsequent child. Tax rates on the absent parent are 20 percent for one child, 30 percent for two children, and 40 percent for three or more children in plans 1 and 3 and 15 percent for one child, 25 percent for two children, and 30 percent for three or more children in plans 2 and 4. Tax rates on custodial parents, not shown in the table, are one half the rates on absent parents. Gross benefits paid out are given in column 1, absent parent and custodial parent tax revenues are shown in columns 2 and 3, AFDC savings are displayed in column 4, and column 5 shows the net savings. Net savings equal the sum of tax revenues from the absent and the custodial parent and AFDC savings minus gross benefits. Column 6 presents the percentage of absent parents who pay as much as or more than the minimum. Column 7 presents the percentage of cases where the tax on the absent parent plus the tax on the custodial parent equals the child support minimum.

Savings range from a low of $39 million to a high of $125 million. These figures are nontrivial. They amount to somewhere between 14 percent and 40 percent of the federal and state expenditures on AFDC in Wisconsin in 1980. However, the estimates of savings are too high, because they assume that 100 percent of the liability of absent parents for child support will be collected. Currently, about 64 percent of this liability is collected. Our best guess is that 80 percent of the potential revenue from absent parents will be collected under the new system. In this case, net savings for the four plans would equal $27 million, $-8 million, $80 million, and $48 million respectively. Finally, the estimates of total savings are too low, because receipt of AFDC benefits is underreported; thus, AFDC savings are underestimated.

What Will Be Demonstrated

The contrast between the dismal reality of the current system and the bright promise of the proposed reform is sufficient to warrant a demonstration of the reform concepts as well as continued work on the cost estimates and program design. The demonstration system consists of four elements: a simple formula for establishing child support obligations, a collection procedure that relies on universal wage withholding, a guaranteed minimum benefit, and a custodial-parent tax. The demonstration will be conducted in two phases. In the first phase, the child support formula and universal wage withholding will be instituted. In the second phase, the minimum benefit and the custodial-parent tax will be added.

The two-phase design will enable us to determine whether the use of automatic wage assignments (that is, the concept of taxation at the source of income) and a simplified normative standard based on the absent parent's ability to pay will improve support obligations sufficiently to warrant the interventions of the second phase, which could prove costly. We already know from past research what the effects of the minimum benefit and the custodial-parent tax are likely to be on costs, caseloads, and poverty. Thus, the two-phase design minimizes fiscal risk, makes change more gradual, and lengthens the time in which we can plan how to administer and how to examine the effects of the minimum benefit and custodial tax.

This chapter devotes more attention to phase one of the demonstration than to phase two because phase one is imminent, and therefore more thought has been devoted to it. Whereas the general outlines of phase two are known, intensive planning for it will not begin until phase one becomes operational.

Phase one of the demonstration focuses on wage withholding. Wage withholding is central, because its success or failure will make or break the program fiscally and because we have no direct evidence on how successful it will be.

In some demonstration counties, universal wage withholding will be achieved by executing a wage assignment in all new cases as soon as the cases are opened. Wisconsin law gives judges and family court commissioners authority to execute wage assignments immediately. A few judges in the state have used this authority. When wage assignments are executed immediately, instead of being used as a response to delinquency, they achieve the effect of automatic wage withholding. The distinction is that between prevention and reaction.

In other demonstration counties, rather than adopting universal wage withholding, we will attempt to improve the response to delinquent payments in order to compare wage withholding not only with average practice under the current reacting system but with the best that is possible under the current system. Current law in Wisconsin provides for a contingent wage assignment in all cases when child support is awarded. The contingent wage assignment gives legal authority to county clerks of courts to initiate a process requiring employers to withhold child support from wages if the absent parent is delinquent for twenty days. Before the wage assignment is issued, the delinquent parent must be notified of his or her right to request a hearing (within ten days); at the hearing, the parent explains why the delinquency exists and why a wage assignment should not be issued. (The clerk cannot impose the wage assignment immediately because, unlike a judge or family court commissioner, the clerk does not have such authority.)

Present law also requires absent parents to make child support payments to the county clerk of courts rather than directly to the custodial parent. Therefore, the appropriate government officials are required by law to know that payments are delinquent. Unfortunately, in practice, delinquencies are not normally detected or responded to for as many as three or four months. There is no routine, computerized response to delinquencies comparable to that of credit card and utility companies. Notification of a right to hearing, the parent's response, and the hearing itself all take time and expend resources. The arrearages built up during the lag are very difficult to collect. The absent parent is likely to use the money for other purposes. Nonpayment begins to be the norm. Experience suggests that, as the lag in detecting a delinquency increases, the likelihood of collecting it decreases.

In the counties where we want to enhance the response to delinquencies, we propose to install a computer system (or modify an existing one) so that these counties have a capability similar to that of credit card and utility companies. When a payment is ten days delinquent, the county will send a letter to the obligor warning him that the process for executing the contingent wage assignment will be initiated if the payment is delinquent for twenty days. When the payment is delinquent for twenty days, the absent parent will be notified that the wage assignment will be executed unless he or she schedules a hearing within ten days. (DHSS is proposing to reduce the delinquency period before the process of executing a wage assignment can begin from twenty days to ten. If the legislature adopts this proposal, the warning letter will be eliminated. Notification of a right to hearing will be sent after ten days of delinquency.)

In still other counties, a taxlike child support formula will be used to set support obligations in all new child support cases. The taxlike formula will operate in one of two ways depending on whether the state legislature acts on a request of the Wisconsin Department of Health and Social Services to give judges and family court commissioners authority to order child support payments as a percentage of income rather than as an absolute amount. We expect that this authority will be enacted. Even if it is not, it is possible under current law to approximate a percentage of income as a basis for child support orders by combining a schedule based on percentage of income with a standard procedure for changes in income.

In principle, it would be desirable to use at least two different formulas. Doing so would enable us to gain some information about the extent to which perceptions about the equity of a given child support formula depend on particular aspects of the formula. However, DHSS officials do not look favorably on the idea of using different child support formulas. Whether we have experimental variations in the child support formula will depend ultimately on the wishes of local judges and family court commissioners.

In the second phase of the demonstration, the minimum benefit and custodial-parent tax will be added, provided that the wage-withholding system and the normative standard collections improved collections sufficiently during phase one. It is assumed that we will add the minimum benefit and custodial tax in only two or three counties; ideally, both wage withholding and the child support formula will already be in effect in these counties. It is also possible that we will vary the benefit level. One critical design issue is how to approximate on a county level the administration of the custodial-parent tax through the state Department of Revenue.

What We Want to Learn

The demonstration should allow us to answer a number of questions: First, what unforeseen administrative problems are associated with the new system? Second, what are the administrative costs of the new system? Third, how effective is universal wage withholding in collecting child support? Fourth, what are the effects of increased collections, the minimum benefit, and the custodial tax on poverty, AFDC costs and caseloads, and the costs of the proposed new system? Fifth, what are the advantages and disadvantages of the new system for absent and custodial parents and their children?

The first question indicates that the demonstration is in part a pilot project. The assumption underlying a pilot project is that the new system is superior to the old. The objective is to iron out the bugs in the new system. There are good reasons for believing that the use of a child support formula and wage withholding will substantially enhance both the equity and the efficiency of collections and that a minimum benefit will substantially reduce welfare costs and caseloads. Consequently, piloting a new system that incorporates these features is warranted. We hypothesize that no unmanageable administrative problems will surface and that responsible administrators will find that the new system is both more equitable and more efficient than the old.

At the same time, the demonstration provides an opportunity to measure the administrative costs of universal wage withholding to employers and government agencies and the administrative costs of paying out the minimum benefit and collecting the custodial tax. We hypothesize that the administrative costs to both the public and private sectors will not change dramatically.

One central question that the first phase of the demonstration is designed to answer concerns the effectiveness of universal wage withholding. It is desirable to compare universal wage withholding both with the operations of the current system and with the optimal operation of the system. There are two reasons for including an enhanced version of the current system (the quick-response variation) in the demonstration. First, there are drawbacks to universal wage withholding. Some consider it an invasion of privacy. It lays an additional administrative burden on employers. As a consequence, some employers may refuse to hire employees with child support obligations or they may fire employees with such obligations. Second, enhancing the existing system so that the first response to delinquent payments is limited to ten days may conceivably improve collections almost as much as universal wage withholding. We hypothesize that quick response will improve collections somewhat and that universal wage withholding will improve collections dramatically.

Measuring the effect of the new system on poverty and on AFDC caseloads and costs is also important, as is measuring the cost of the proposed new system. We have already developed simulation estimates of these effects. But, extrapolating from actual experience will give us an independent estimate of these effects and enhance the credibility of the enterprise as a whole. We hypothesize that universal wage withholding, the child support formula, and the minimum benefit will all lead to substantial decreases in poverty and AFDC caseloads and costs and that the system as a whole will lead to modest decreases in general revenue costs.

Finally, the demonstration is unique in measuring the effects on parental attitudes and interactions. Under the current system, both absent and custodial parents often feel that they have been treated inequitably. The adversarial nature of the system often exacerbates existing tensions between former spouses, and in some cases it worsens relations between one or both parents and the child. The demonstration will enable us to examine whether the new system can improve matters in this domain. We hypothesize that use of a child support standard will lead parents to perceive the system as more equitable, that it will therefore decrease quarrels about child support between ex-spouses, that universal wage withholding will increase visits by the absent parent to the child, and that it will decrease the jailing of absent parents. Finally, we expect that both universal wage withholding and the minimum benefit will increase the financial security of the custodial parent.

Data Required and Data Sources

The data required to address the five questions that we want to answer come from different sources and therefore have different costs. Data on unforeseen administrative problems associated with the new system will be generated as the demonstration proceeds. We propose to interview local officials involved in the operation of the new system.

Ascertaining administrative costs of the new system will require additional effort. A new accounting system will have to be developed. Furthermore, employers and related government agents, such as sheriffs, will have to be interviewed to determine how much time they spend on child support activities under the old and new systems.

In order to determine how much more effective the new system is than the old in collecting child support, we will need data on child support payments and child support orders under the old and new systems. Data on payments and awards can be obtained in most cases from records in the office of the county clerk of courts. Although the law requires that all payments be made through the court, some payments are made directly. Telephone interviews will probably be necessary to check on direct payments. In counties that adopt our new child support formula, child support orders will be expressed as a percentage of income rather than as an absolute amount. This means that we will need information on the person's total income in order to measure how much he or she should be paying. Such information should be available at the county clerk's office, because, where the new formula is adopted, payers will be required to file copies of their income tax returns with the clerk of courts. Other useful data that can be obtained from the records of the county clerk of courts include enforcement actions, such as wage assignments and jailings, and the date of the court order. It would also be useful to have demographic data on income, marital status, and so forth for the analysis of payments. Because these factors affect payments, including them in the analysis will sharpen our estimates of the effects of wage withholding.

Data on the effects of the new system on AFDC costs and caseloads can be obtained from the state's computer reporting network (CRN). Data on the new system can be obtained from the CRN and the fiscal accounting system of the demonstration itself.

In order to use the demonstration to project effects of the new system on poverty, we need data on income, which can come either from income tax data or from individual interviews. By obtaining social security numbers from the clerk of courts records, we can get data from income tax returns in most cases. Where we cannot we will have to use telephone or personal interviews.

Finally, data on the parents' attitudes and interactions with each other and with their children will be obtained from telephone or personal interviews. The data and sources needed to address the five questions are summarized in Figure 1.

Evaluation Design

This section deals only with how to measure the effects of the demonstration on collections. The same logic extends to the other effects that we wish to measure. To simplify the discussion, we proceed in the first two subsections as if the only difference between the old and new system were universal wage withholding. In the first subsection, we discuss the arguments for and against a classical experimental design. In the second subsection, we describe an alternative evaluation design that, while less robust than the classic experimental design, will afford us the kind of empirical data on which sound policy decisions can be based. In the design, we attempt to balance reliability of results with cost.

A Classical Experimental Design. An essential element of an experiment is random assignment to treatment or control status. In the case of the child support demonstration, use of a classic experimental design would require the judge or some agent of the court to assign some absent parents to the universal wage withholding group and others to the current system, completely at random. The rationale for random assignment is that it is the only way of ensuring that any observed difference between the treatment and the control group is the result of treatment.

Figure 1. Questions, Data Needed, and Sources

Question	Data Needed	Source
Unforeseen administrative problems	Real program experience	Personal interviews of local officials
Administrative costs	Costs to employees and all public-sector agencies	Accounting system plus interviews of local officials
Effects on collections	Payments/orders	Clerk of court records Wisconsin income tax returns Telephone interviews
Effects on AFDC costs and caseloads	County AFDC costs and caseloads	State computer reporting network
New system costs	Income	Telephone interviews
Poverty	Income	Telephone interviews
Effects on parents' attitudes and interactions with each other and with children	Perception of equity Visitation Fights Security	Telephone interviews

However, random assignment of individuals within a jurisdiction to different treatments poses some problems. First, it is possible that doing so would not be legal. Second, even if it is legal, it will probably be difficult to convince judges to participate if random assignment is involved. Third, it seems likely that the demonstration would be less useful as a pilot program if random assignment were used. Fourth, for all these reasons, some key state officials have already indicated that they think it absurd to consider random assignment of individuals.

Random assignment of counties to experimental or control status would be pointless. Too few counties are involved to ensure that there will be no differences between experimental and control counties except for those caused by the experiment. Random assignment works only when large numbers are involved. If you flip a coin only ten times, it is unlikely that you will get five heads and five tails. However, if you flip the coin 500 times, you will get close to 250 heads and 250 tails.

In view of these drawbacks to the classic experimental design, we developed an alternative, which is described in the next section. Note, however, that in the evaluation of the minimum benefit and custodial-parent tax the first two arguments against random assignment — legality and judges — do not pertain.

A Before-After and Cross-Site Design. The demonstration of the new system will take place in certain counties. To evaluate its effects, we will compare collection effectiveness in the counties with the new system to collection effectiveness in the same counties before the new system was installed and to collection effectiveness in similar counties with the current system during the same time period. The weakness of restricting evaluation to before-after comparison in the counties with the new system is that something else besides the collection system may have changed. For example, an improvement in the economy could lead to improvements in child support collections that would be attributed to the new system if only a before-after comparison was used. By using matched comparison sites as well, we can control for improvements in the economy and other general changes that affect all counties alike over time.

The weakness of using only cross-site comparisons is that the counties may differ in other ways besides the presence or absence of treatment. For example, higher-income counties are likely to have a better record of child support payments. Matching counties perfectly is likely to prove difficult. By using historical data for each site, we can control for differences across sites.

Of course, even the combination of before-after and cross-site comparisons does not assure an unbiased estimate of the treatment. For example, if a major plant closed in a comparison site, the child support collections at that site might be lower than they were at the demonstration site. Changes peculiar to the demonstration or comparison counties will confound estimates of the treatment effect. The best protection against this eventuality is to have as many different sites and to collect as much historical data as we can afford.

There is no scientific way of ascertaining exactly how many counties should be included in the demonstration or how much historical data should be collected precisely because of the question of cost. The greater the number of counties included and the more data collected, the more costly the demonstration will be. The recommendations given here reflect our desire both to develop the information that we need in order to answer the questions that the demonstration is designed to address and to minimize costs. Our recommendations (especially with regard to counties) are tentative for two additional reasons: First, before we finalize the design, we will consult with several experts in experimental design. Second, our ability to carry out any design that requires counties to adopt particular features of the demonstration will depend on the cooperation of county officials.

For the before-after comparison, we recommend that payment data be collected in all designated counties for two years before the demonstration begins and for at least two years after it starts. With respect to the cross-site comparisons, we have five recommendations: First, four counties should adopt universal wage withholding. Second, two separate counties should adopt the quick-response variation. Third, at least two but no more than three of the wage-withholding counties and one of the quick-response counties should adopt a reformed child support standard. Fourth, one county should use the reformed child support standard without any change in collection strategy. Fifth, at least three control counties should continue to operate as they do now. If these recommendations are adopted, data will be obtained in a minimum of ten counties.

The rationale for the cross-site experimental design is this: First, the wage-withholding feature is the most important behavioral focus of phase one of the demonstration. Hence, this intervention is used in four counties. Quick response is much less important. The child support formula falls somewhere in between. We expect differences in standards to have only a small effect on collections. However, differences in standards may have a large effect on perceptions of equity. Therefore, we will introduce a normative standard in at least four and perhaps five different counties.

The large overlap between standards and the other features is justified by the fact that the independent effects of the child support formula and either wage withholding or quick response on collections can be separated out algebraically in counties that have both. The effect of the formula on collections will be primarily through the amount owed, while the effect of wage withholding and quick response will be exclusively on the percentage of the obligation paid. (Presumably, as the obligation decreases, the percentage of it that will be paid increases. We should be able to measure this potential effect nonexperimentally and control for it.)

How Long Should the Demonstration Last?

The longer the demonstration goes on, the more we can learn from it. A short design limits the experimental costs, but our understanding of the concepts of the reform that results would be limited. Our recommendation is that the demonstration should last two years.

At least two studies have found that payment behavior varies over time: Eckhardt (1968) found in Dane County, Wisconsin, that the proportion of absent fathers who paid support declined steadily. In contrast, Chambers (1979) found in Genessee County, Michigan, that the opposite was the case. The differences appear to be attributable to differences in child support enforcement in the two counties and to learned behavior on the part of the absent fathers. Nonpayment was not punished in Dane County in the early 1960s in Genessee County it was. Apparently, the men learned this and behaved accordingly. In any case, because payments can vary over time, it is essential to see how the effectiveness of wage withholding varies over time. Two years appear to be the minimum. Three years would be preferable.

Moreover, wage withholding is complicated by job changing. Each time an absent parent changes jobs, the parent must tell the child support enforcement agency that he or she has a new employer and the new employer that his or her child support payment must be withheld from his or her wages. The longer the demonstration lasts, the more absent parents will change jobs. Again, at least two years seem to be the minimum required if we are to gain experience with how well wage withholding holds up over time in the face of job shifts.

A third reason for extending the demonstration beyond one year is that new administrative processes take time to shake down. It is possible that the counties with universal wage withholding will do worse at first because the procedures are new. Or, they may do better as a result of the excitement generated by being part of a demonstration. In either case, because we want to measure how wage withholding works routinely, the first six months or so of operations should receive less weight than the next year or so. Similarly, there could be adverse effects on employee morale as the demonstration draws to a close. Consequently, if we allow for six months of possible wind-down effects at the end, a two-year demonstration would give us a minimum of twelve months that would approximate normal functioning. A three-year demonstration would give us two years of routine functioning.

The monetary costs of running and evaluating the first phase of the demonstration for three rather than two years are not very large. The costs of operating the demonstration should be negative in the sense that we expect the experimental counties to improve their collections. Indeed, the chief costs may be the costs of forgone enhanced collections caused by postponing implementation of the new system in the control counties. However, since we are not certain how much better the new system will work in practice, this cost should be borne.

The same arguments apply on the benefit side. It will take time for beneficiaries to gain information about and experience with the new child support system. One year is a very short time. However, two practical considerations led us to recommend evaluation of only one year of experience with the benefit side. First, key state officials want results by 1986. Second, requesting a funder to support an evaluation for more than three years is probably not feasible in these tight fiscal times. If a longer evaluation is justified, the results after two years of operation (including one year of the benefit system) will amply justify it.

Should the Demonstration Be Limited to New Cases?

The easiest way of piloting the new system would be to confine its application to new cases. When cases appear before the court, wage withholding orders would be issued as a matter of course. To effect wage withholding orders in old cases would require informing the absent parent, ascertaining where he or she was employed, and notifying the employer.

Including old cases in the demonstration would raise several other problems. First, it is unlikely that the old cases could be analyzed together with the new cases. The treatment that the new cases receive will be quite different. Consider the use of the child support standards. If the standard is applied to old cases, it will require changing the amount of child support owed as well as the manner of collecting it. The effects of changing the amount of support owed at a later time may be different from the effects of establishing support at the same level from the outset. If the standard is not applied, then old and new cases will differ in the obligation owed. So, any gains in sample size would be illusory. Second, it may be more difficult to persuade jurisdictions to participate if we include the old cases. The difficulty is apt to increase if we wish to apply the child support formula and therefore readjust old orders. Third, including old cases may overtax the administrative capabilities of the participating counties, at least in the early stages of the demonstration.

There are two arguments for including old cases in the new system. First, if we take only new cases, we will gain no experience of what is involved in introducing the fully implemented form. Under the proposed reform, any custodial parent may apply for the public child support benefit. Such an application brings both the custodial and the absent parent into the new system. Consequently, many old cases will be incorporated into the system. Thus, forgoing the opportunity to examine what this entails is no minor matter. Second, if we take only new cases, we will learn nothing about the effectiveness of wage withholding on the child support collected from parents who have been living apart from their children for more than a few years. As already noted, some research indicates that nonpayment becomes increasingly serious over time. Consequently, taking only new cases may omit the toughest cases from the analysis.

Perhaps the best resolution is to include only new cases in the first part of the demonstration and then to phase in old cases after six or nine months. For evaluation purposes, we will proceed as if only new cases will be included during the first year. If old cases are included during the second year, we will collect additional data at that time.

The Nature and Size of Sample

The kind of cases on which we want to collect data depends on whether just new or old and new child support cases are included in the demonstration. If only new cases are included, then only new cases should be selected for controls. Thus, when we get payment records for the twenty-four months prior to the start of the demonstration, we will want payment records for only the cases that began during that period. Further, when we analyze only nine months of past demonstration experience, we will use only the first nine months of data for the controls. If we used old cases as well, we will have up to two years of data on the previous payment experience of the old cases selected for the demonstration. At the control sites, the way the old cases were chosen for inclusion in the treatment would be replicated to obtain a set of controls.

The size of the sample depends on how much money we are willing to spend to get good estimates of the effects of wage withholding. Estimates improve as the sample size increases, but they also cost more money. However, once the sample size reaches the thousands, the cost per additional case and the precision of the estimates remain relatively constant. When the sample is very large—say 10,000—increasing the sample size does not improve the estimates to any measurable degree.

How much estimates improve with increases in sample size can be measured by a statistical formula. The quality of the estimates is measured in terms of two things: how small an effect is programmatically significant, and how certain we want to be of detecting that effect. In the context of child support collections, the size of the effect translates into how small an increase in child support payments warrants adoption of the reform program. If collections in the reform counties do not increase by at least 20 percent, the second phase of the demonstration might be in jeopardy from a policy perspective. For example, if wage withholding increases payments only by 5 percent, it might as well not increase payments at all, since we would not recommend going to universal wage withholding merely to increase payments by 5 percent. The point is important, because we would need a much bigger sample to detect a 5 percent increase in payments than we would need to detect a 20 percent increase. Suppose that we want to be able to say with scientific confidence that payments increased by 20 percent. What size sample would be required for that? Answering the question, How likely is it that the true increase is 20 percent? involves a trade-off between cost and experimental certitude. Do we want our chance to be one out of two, three out of four, or ninety-five out of hundred? The more certain we want to be of detecting an effect of a particular size, the bigger the sample must be.

Another consideration is how many ways we want to split the sample. It is likely that we will want to do separate analyses for AFDC and non-AFDC cases. Will we also want to disaggregate the results by demographic factors? Past research indicates that payment patterns differ substantially by race. At the same time, analyses of selected subsamples necessitate a large aggregate sample. To get a sufficiently large sample of blacks in Wisconsin will require us to involve particular areas, such as Milwaukee or Racine and Kenosha, and probably also to oversample blacks in these areas. In some cases, it will also be desirable to disaggregate by county. This would enable us to analyze the effects of different child support formulas on perceptions of equity. Other desirable disaggregations include marital status of the custodial parent (never married, separated, divorced, remarried) and residence of the absent parent (in or out of state). To summarize, the larger the sample size, the smaller the empirical effect we will be able to detect; moreover, a large sample size will enable us to disaggregate the analysis in important policy-relevant ways.

On the cost side, there are very big differences depending on the data source. Telephone interviews are quite expensive. Based on previous experience with the Wisconsin Survey Lab, which is far cheaper than alternative professional survey organizations, our tentative estimate is $50 per interview. (We currently lean toward conducting the survey ourselves, which could reduce the cost, but for budget purposes we have assumed a cost of $50 per interview.) The next most expensive data are those on payments and orders collected from the clerk of courts. Our tentative estimate is $4 per case. The cost could be lower if more counties than we have assumed prove to have computerized records. Finally, the cost of obtaining CRN data is practically zero.

With respect to court records, we propose the sampling scheme described in Table 2. There would be a total of 9,000 cases, 7,000 from the experimental counties, and 2,000 from the control counties. Five-sevenths of the cases drawn from experimental counties would be postexperimental cases.

This is a very big sample. It would give us a 95 percent chance of detecting a 10 percent increase in payments for only half the sample. We have several reasons for making our sample quite large: the small cost of data collection, the importance of getting good estimates of the effects of withholding on collections, and the probability that we will want to disaggregate in more ways than by dividing the sample in half.

We plan to collect data twice for each case. We will collect data on cases that began in 1981 and 1982 during the summer of 1983 and once again in summer 1985. For cases that began after July 1, 1983, we will collect data in the summer of 1984 and again in summer 1985. By waiting until summer 1984 to collect data on cases beginning after July 1983, we will get payment data for up to one year in order to prepare a report by the end of 1984. Although we do not anticipate negative results, the report will be prepared in time to permit last-minute postponement or even cancellation of phase two if the results of phase one are sufficiently negative. Data collection during summer 1985 will give us an additional year of payment data on experimental cases and an additional two years of payment data on preexperimental cases. The timeline for data collection and analysis is displayed in Figure 2. However, because telephone interviews are costly, we are tentatively recommending a much smaller sample, 900 cases. The sample will be drawn at random from the court sample, one case for every ten in each cell of Table 2. Each case involves two interviews, one of the absent parent and one of the custodial parent. Thus, if both parents are interviewed once, 900 cases lead to 1,800 interviews.

As Figure 2 indicates, the telephone interviews for the cases that began before July 1, 1983 will be conducted late in 1983. Telephone interviews cannot begin until after the court records sample is drawn, coded, and put on tape. Telephone interviews for cases that begin after July 1, 1983 will not be

Table 2. Number of Court Cases Sampled by Time of Case Opening and Type of County

Date Cases Begin	Four Wage-Withholding Counties[a]	Two Quick-Response Counties[b]	County with Child Support Standard Only	Three Control Counties	Total
July 1, 1981–June 30, 1982	600	300	100	250	1,250
July 1, 1982–June 30, 1983	600	300	100	250	1,250
July 1, 1983–May 1983	3,000	2,600	500	1,500	6,500
Total	4,200	2,100	700	2,000	9,000

[a] Two or three of these also have child support standard.
[b] One of these also has child support standard.

Figure 2. Timeline for Data Collection and Analysis

	1983	1984	1985	1986
	J J A S O N D	J F M A M J J A S O N D	J F M A M J J A S O N D	J F M A M
Predemonstration Court Records	C C C P P A A R[F]		C C C P P A A R A A A	A
Predemonstration Telephone Interviews		C C C C P A A R[F]		
Postdemonstration Court Records		C C C P A A R[F] A R[F] P	C C C P P A A R[F]	C C C P P A A R[P] A A A R[F]
Postdemonstration Telephone Interviews		C C C C P P A A R[F]		C C C P P A A R[F]
Computer Reporting Network Pre and Post		C P P A A R[P] A A R[F]		C P P A A A R[P] A A R[F]
Administrator Interviews	C C C	C P A R[P] C C	C P A R[P]	C C P A R[F]

Note: Predemonstration refers to court cases that begin prior to the start of the demonstration.
Postdemonstration refers to court cases that begin after the start of the demonstration.
C indicates that data are collected during the month.
P indicates that data are prepared for analysis during the month.
A indicates that data are analyzed during the month.
R indicates that a report is presented. The P and F superscripts indicate whether the report is preliminary or final.

conducted until late 1984 in order to allow up to one year's experience with the new system. The second round of telephone interviews conducted late in 1985 will serve two purposes. First, it will give us an additional year of data on how parents behave under the collection parts of the new system and on how they feel about them. Second, it will give us the first data on how the minimum benefit and custodial-parent tax affect custodial parents. The sample for the second round of telephone interviews will be half as large as that for the first round, namely 450 cases. However, all cases in sites with the minimum benefit and custodial tax will be included. The total number of telephone interviews therefore comes to 2,700.

The CRN sample will consist of all cases in the court record sample that appear in the CRN sample plus everyone else in the CRN sample who resides in an experimental or a control county. Because the CRN sample is the cheapest and quickest source to access, we will draw our samples from the CRN on three different occasions, summer 1983 for predemonstration cases and summer 1984 and winter 1985 for both pre- and postdemonstration cases.

Local administrators will be interviewed immediately after the program begins and again at periodic intervals throughout the course of the demonstration. Most of the officials interviewed will be visited in person only once or twice. For purposes of budgeting, we have assumed that we will conduct no more than 200 personal interviews.

Statistical Analysis

This section focuses on the approach that will be used to analyze the major experimental outcomes. Although some of the research, such as the study of administrators' reactions to the new system and the administrative cost study, will not involve the kinds of statistical analyses described here, most will. For the sake of the exposition, assume that the demonstration is conducted in the calendar year 1983 and that wage withholding and quick response are the only variations. The following regression will be run to ascertain the effect of universal wage withholding on child support collections:

$$\frac{P}{O} = a_0 = a_1 Tr_1 + a_2 1981 + a_3 1982 + \sum_{i=0} b_i S_i + \sum_i c_i Z_i,$$

where P is child support payments (probably per year), o is child support order (probably per year), Tr_1 is sites with universal wage withholding, Tr_2 is sites with quick response to delinquency, 1981 is a dummy variable for cases that began in 1981, 1982 is a dummy variable for cases that began in 1982, S_i is a dummy variable equal to one for the ith site, Z_i is a set of demographic variables that include income, race, and age, and a_0, a_1, a_2, a_3, a_4, b_i, and c_i are parameters to be estimated.

The parameters of most interest are a_1 and a_2. The former measures the impact on collections of universal wage withholding. The latter measures the effect of quick response to delinquency. The difference between a_1 and a_2 measures the effect of wage withholding vis-à-vis an enhanced version of the current system.

The effects on poverty, costs, caseloads, parental attitudes, and parental interactions with each other and their children would be measured in the same way. Only the dependent variable would change. The effects of different standards on these dependent variables would be captured both by dummy variables and by variables measuring support orders in relation to income.

References

Chambers, D. L. *Making Fathers Pay: The Enforcement of Child Support.* Chicago: University of Chicago Press, 1979.

Danziger, S. *Children in Poverty: The Truly Needy Who Fall Through the Safety Net.* Discussion Paper 680-81. Madison, Wisc.: Institute for Research on Poverty, 1981.

Eckhardt, K. "Deviance, Visibility, Legal Action: The Duty to Support." *Social Problems,* 1968, *15,* 470-477.

Garfinkel, I., and Melli, M. *Child Support: Weaknesses of the Old and Features of a Proposed New System.* Madison, Wisc.: Institute for Research on Poverty, 1982.

Moynihan, D. P. "Welfare Reforms' 1971-72 Defeat: A Historic Loss." *Journal of the Institute of Socioeconomic Studies,* 1981, *6,* 1-20.

U.S. Department of Commerce. *Child Support and Alimony: 1978.* Current Population Reports, Special Study Series P-23, No. 112. Washington, D.C.: Bureau of the Census, U.S. Department of Commerce, 1981.

Yee, L. M. "What Really Happens in Child Support Cases: An Empirical Study of Establishment and Enforcement of Child Support Orders in the Denver District Court." *Denver Law Journal,* 1979, *57,* 21-68.

Irwin Garfinkel is professor and director, School of Social Work, and research fellow, Institute for Research on Poverty, University of Wisconsin, Madison.

Thomas Corbett is research specialist, Institute for Research on Poverty, University of Wisconsin, Madison.

The perennial problem of comparing apples to oranges finds hope for relief by assessing the preferences of decision makers and stakeholders in public policy decisions.

Economic Transformations of Nonmonetary Benefits in Program Evaluation

Stuart S. Nagel

This chapter discusses some new ways of handling multidimensional trade-offs in policy evaluation. It places the emphasis on psychological monetizing by means of paired comparisons. The problem of multidimensional trade-offs goes to the heart of political science if that discipline is defined as the study of who gets and who should get what, when, how, and why or as the study of the authoritative allocation of things of value. Any allocation system is likely to run into the problem of multiple criteria in allocating money, land, labor, capital, or any other thing of value. It is a rare situation where only one criterion determines who gets what when resources are allocated to persons, groups, or places. If there are multiple criteria, it is likely that one of the objects to which things of value could be allocated will score relatively high on one criterion but not so high on another. Moreover, it is likely that multiple criteria are expressed in different units of measurement. Determining how to allocate in light of multiple criteria measured in different ways is the essence of the problem of handling multidimensional trade-offs in policy evaluation.

Three new ways of handling multidimensional trade-offs are discussed in this chapter: incremental analysis, percentaging analysis, and paired-comparison psychological monetizing. The first two methods are covered in detail elsewhere, but they are summarized here to illustrate their similarities and differences. Nagel (1983a) examines incremental analysis. Nagel (1983b) discusses percentaging analysis; Edwards and Newman (1982), Saaty (1980), and Keeney and Raiffa (1976) examine alternative methods. The third method, paired-comparison monetizing, compares various nonmonetary benefits with various dollar amounts. The essence of the method involves finding the turning point in a series of paired comparisons. The turning point is the point at which the decision maker moves from valuing the nonmonetary benefits higher than the dollar amounts to valuing the dollar amounts higher than the nonmonetary benefits. Once the turning point has been determined, the information about it can be converted into an equation that can be used to translate nonmonetary benefits into dollars while taking diminishing returns into consideration. The resulting translation can then enable decision makers to resolve multidimensional trade-offs, because the translation converts all the criteria or goals into monetary values. However, these values are not the kind of monetary values referred to by economists when they discuss actual or contrived marketplaces. These are monetary values only in terms of the psychological preferences of those who are making the allocation decisions or otherwise choosing among alternative public policies. On the general subject of converting nonmonetary values into dollars, the reader can consult Rhoads (1980), Chase (1968), and Thompson (1980). Baumol (1977) and Sellin and Wolfgang (1964) examine the issue of converting nonmonetary values into absolute or relative utility.

Using nonmonetary measures, such as satisfaction units, for goals is no problem if all the goals can be measured with the same nonmonetary unit. Likewise, having multiple measures is no problem if one policy scores higher than the others on all the goals. We have a problem only when we have a combination of multidimensionality and trade-offs in which one policy is better on one goal, while another policy is better on another.

The Nature of the Problem and Nonmonetizing Alternatives

Public policy evaluation involves the determination of which of various alternative government policies or decisions is best for achieving a given set of goals. To make such a determination, it is often helpful to express the goals in a common unit of measurement, such as money. To illustrate, we can imagine the case of having to decide which of two health policies is better: one that trains thirty students and treats ten patients, or one that trains twenty students and treats eighteen patients. The basic information involved in such a decision is shown in Table 1 in the two columns giving raw scores. If a dollar value could be placed on training students and treating patients, one could determine the dollar value of each policy, then choose the policy with the higher dollar value.

Incremental analysis is one alternative to monetizing the goal variables. Incremental analysis converts the problem just outlined into one of determining

Table 1. Three Methods for Dealing with Multidimensional Trade-offs

Raw Score Increments

Policy	Students Trained (S)	Patients Treated (P)
Policy A (X_1)	30	10
Policy B (X_2)	20	18
Total (Whole)	50	28
Difference (Increment)	+10S > >	− 8P ?

Part-Whole Percentaging

Policy	Students Trained	Patients Treated	Unweighted Sum	Weighted Sum $W = 2$
Policy A (X_1)	60%	36%	96%	132%
Policy B (X_2)	40%	64%	104%	168%
Total (Whole)	100%	100%	200%	300%

Threshold: $W60 + 36 = W40 + 64$. ∴ $W^* = 1.40$

Paired Comparison Monetizing

Policy	Students Trained $Y = (S)^{.92}$	Patients Treated $Y = (P)^{.90}$	Sum
Policy A (X_1)	$22.85	$ 7.94	$30.79
Policy B (X_2)	$15.74	$13.48	$29.22
Total	$38.59	$21.42	$60.01
Threshold	(Z_1)	(Z_2)	ΣΥ

whether one prefers an extra (or incremental) ten students trained or an extra eight patients treated. If decision makers prefer ten extra students trained to eight extra patients treated, then policy A is better, since it provides the extra students trained. If decision makers prefer the eight patients to the ten students, then policy B is better, since it provides the extra patients treated. The key subjective matter when the problem is stated this way is which of the two increments or differences is preferred. The essence of the incremental method is summarized in the *Difference (Increment)* row of Table 1. The method has the advantage of transforming the raw data less than the other two methods. However, that can become a disadvantage if the raw data are difficult to work with. (To be strictly accurate, the proper comparison is not between on extra ten students trained and an extra eight patients treated but between an extra ten students trained over a base of twenty students and an extra eight patients treated over a base of ten patients. An extra ten students does not mean much if the first policy generates 210 students and the second policy generates 200. In other words, the utility of an increment diminishes as we have more to begin with or more to build on.)

Percentaging analysis is another alternative to monetizing the goals variables. It involves transforming the scores on each goal variable into part-whole percentages that can be added or subtracted as pure numbers. In the case that we are considering, policy A has a score of 60 percent on students trained—30/(30 + 50)—while policy B has a score of 40 percent—20/50. On patients treated, policy A gets a score of 36 percent, and policy B gets a score of 64 percent. If training students and treating patients are equally important, then policy A has a total score of 96 percent, and policy B has a total score of 104 percent. The key subjective matter when the problem is stated in this way lies in deciding whether the relative weight or value of students trained or of patients treated is more or less than the threshold value. The threshold value is determined by setting the weighted total score of the two policies equal. The resulting equation reads $W(.60) + .36 = W(.40) + .64$. Solving for W or the relative weight yields a threshold value of 1.4. Thus, if the value of training one student is worth 1.4 times more than the value of treating one patient, then policy A is to be preferred. However, if the value of training one student is 1.4 times less than the value of treating one patient, then policy B is better. The essence of the percentaging method is summarized in the *Weighted Sum* Column of Table 1. Percentaging analysis involves a compromise between working with the raw data and trying to transform the nonmonetary benefits into dollars.

We could make the problem that we have been considering more complicated by adding additional goals and additional policies. For example, we could add the goal of dollar costs. If we do, and if we suppose that policy A costs $70 and policy B costs $50, the incremental analysis approach reduces the problem to one of answering the question, Which is to be preferred: ten extra students trained or eight extra patients treated and $30 saved? If the ten-student increment is preferred, then policy A is the better. If the eight-patient,

$30 increment is preferred, then policy B is the better. The percentaging analysis is also capable of handling another goal. On the dollar cost goal, policy A receives a part-whole percentage of 70/120 or 58 percent, and policy B receives a part-whole percentage of 50/120 or 42 percent. The part-whole percentages are then subtracted from the unweighted sum of 38 percent, and policy B receives an unweighted sum of 62 percent. To make these results more meaningful, we need to weight or multiply the three percentages of policy A and the three percentages of policy B by the relative weights of the three goals. Determining the relative weight of one student trained to one monetary unit would enable us to show the decision maker the monetary value of one student trained. However, the relative weighting method is a more difficult method for monetizing nonmonetary benefits than the method that will be proposed here, because the relative weighting method is almost the same as directly asking the monetary value of training one student.

We could add two more policy alternatives: to choose neither, or to choose both. When there are four alternatives, the incremental analysis approach requires comparing policy A with policy B, as we have already done. The winner in that comparison must then be compared with policy C — doing neither. The winner in that comparison must then be compared with policy D — doing both. The policy that remains after N-1 paired comparisons is the overall winner. Under percentaging analysis, each of the four policies receives three percentages for each of the three goals. The winning policy is the one that has the highest weighted sum of percentages. For the sake of simplicity, the rest of this chapter assumes that we have only two mutually exclusive policies and two goals. However, one advantage of monetizing is that it can deal more readily with multiple goals and multiple policies than either the incremental or the percentaging approach. The bottom half of Table 1 deals with paired-comparison monetizing, which the rest of this chapter will examine.

The literature describes a number of other methods for dealing with multidimensional measurements. They all have flaws. For example, the analytical hierarchy process approach (Saaty, 1980) seeks to reduce all relations to a one-to-nine scale, and it cannot deal with negative goals. Moreover, it is far more complicated than necessary, and it is arbitrary in dealing with inconsistencies. Multiattribute utility theory (Edwards and Newman, 1982) is highly arbitrary in other ways: It depends on such concepts as plausible maximum and plausible minimum, it does not take diminishing returns into consideration, and it works with percentages that do not total 100 percent. The electre method (Bui, 1981) overemphasizes the rank order of each policy on each goal in an unduly complicated system of paired comparisons. The multiobjective programming perspective (Zeleny, 1982) involves numerous highly complicated and conflicting methods, such as goal programming, which deals with each goal sequentially, not with all goals simultaneously. Finally, the conjoint measures method (Grether and Wilde, 1974) establishes minimum cutoff levels on each goal variable. It thereby eliminates some policies that do not satisfy the minima, but it cannot select a single alternative from among a number of competing policies.

Paired Comparisons of Benefits and Dollars

A third approach to dealing with the problems that we have considered is to try to convert students trained and patients treated into dollars. Normally, this is quite difficult to do in a meaningful way. Economists tend to monetize by looking for relevant prices in the marketplace, reasoning by analogy to the marketplace, or creating artificial or imaginary markets. One could try to determine the value of students trained by seeing how much it costs to train a student. However, that tells us only the cost of training a student, not the value or benefits derived from training a student. Likewise, determining how much it costs to treat a patient does not tell us the value of the benefits derived from treating a patient.

To determine the benefits of training, we could try to see how much more an individual with the training is capable of earning than the same kind of individual without the training. However, many of the benefits may not be monetary; for example, neither the prestige of the new position nor the satisfaction that comes from the creativity associated with the new position is monetary. Likewise, seeing how much more a rehabilitated patient can earn does not capture the patient's satisfaction at no longer having the handicap.

Traditional monetizing thus tends to ignore important benefits to which it is difficult to assign a dollar value. It also tends to place more emphasis on the values manifested in the marketplace than on the values of the relevant decision makers who may price student training or patient treatment at a higher or lower value than the marketplace does. For the economics approach to monetizing, see Gramlich (1981), Sugden and Williams (1978), and Mishan (1976). The concept of relevant decision maker varies with the specific decision-making problem. In the situation that we are considering here, the relevant decision maker may be the dean of a university medical school who is trying to decide between two different affirmative action programs. One program will cause more students to be trained and fewer patients to be treated than the other. In the dean's mind, one student trained may be worth more than one patient treated because the dean is thinking not of what a doctor can earn in the medical marketplace but that a black doctor can act as a role for black students, provide needed medical service in the black community, and help the school to comply with U.S. Department of Health and Human Services affirmative action requirements.

For these reasons, we need a method of monetizing that reflects the values of the relevant decision makers or stakeholders, including the extemely subjective values that are generally difficult and often impossible to monetize. The relevant decision makers are those who have the responsibility for deciding the choice or allocation problem under consideration, such as which of the two policies compared in Table 1 is to be adopted. The relevant decision maker or decision makers may or may not include the people who will receive the benefits or suffer the costs of the decisions being made.

A method of monetizing that is capable of meeting these criteria is the method of paired comparisons between benefits and dollars. This method involves presenting the relevant decision makers with a series of questions, such as the following: First, which would you rather have, $1,000 or ten students trained? If the decision maker says ten students trained, then the next question should decrease the number of students trained and increase the number of dollars. For example: Which would you rather have, $2,000 or seven students trained? If the decision maker still says seven students trained, then the number of students trained should be decreased and the number of dollars should be increased. For example: Which would you rather have, $6,000 or two students trained? If the decision maker says at this point that $6,000 is more valuable, then we can infer that the decision maker's turning point is somewhere between $6,000 and $2,000 on the one hand and between seven and two students on the other. The interpolated midpoints between the pairs of boundaries are $4,000 and 4.5 students.) If the decision maker had said in response to the first question that saving $1,000 was worth more than ten students trained, then the next question should have decreased the number of dollars saved and increased the number of students trained. The questioner should have kept decreasing the number of dollars and increasing the number of students until the turning point was reached.) To return to our sample case, the boundaries between $6,000 and $2,000 and between seven students and two students could be narrowed by asking additional questions. We could ask approximately the same questions about patients. That is, we could start by asking the decision maker, Which would you rather have, $1,000 or ten patients treated? When we get to the turning point, we may find that the midpoints between the boundaries are $5,000 and six patients.

In most policy evaluation problems, there are multiple decision makers or many people whose values count. A sample of these people could be asked a series of questions like those just outlined. The midpoints could then be averaged in order to determine an average turning point for students trained and patients treated. Guilford (1954) examines the use of paired comparisons in measuring attitudes. Henerson and others (1978) discuss attitude measurement in program evaluation. Rose and Prell (1955), Phillips and Votey (1981), and Sellin and Wolfgang (1964) have all discussed the use of attitude measurement and interpolation in monetizing the seriousness of particular crimes. Interpolation scores crimes in terms of their seriousness. It notes the fines levied for crimes that have them and then interpolates or extrapolates to other crimes. One alternative is to note the dollar amounts in crimes involving theft and to interpolate or extrapolate these values to other crimes.

If the decision maker has a turning-point equation of $4,000 and 4.5 students, we still do not know why he or she placed that dollar value on that number of students. The decision maker may be the dean of a medical school, and policies A and B may be two different affirmative action programs. The decision maker may be thinking of having to please the affirmative action requirements of the U.S. Department of Health and Human Services. He or she may want to provide more black role models for black undergraduates and high school students. He or she may be thinking of the need to provide the black community with medical service, of how much the students will contribute to the medical school as alumni, or of the number of black medical students the school already has. For decision-making purposes, these considerations are not important. Two things are important: first, that we have asked the right decision maker, namely one whose values count in determining what action will be taken; second, that we have asked the right questions, so that we are getting meaningful answers. The paired-comparison approach seems to be a better way of asking meaningful questions than the direct approach, What is the dollar value to you of a student trained? It also seems to be more meaningful than approaches involving artificial lotteries, which most people find difficult to grasp.

Transforming the Threshold Equation to Consider Diminishing Returns

What do we do with the data we have just generated? The turning-point or threshold equation is $4,000 = 4.5$ students. In theory, we could divide both sides of that equation by 4.5 in order to deduce that one student trained is worth $889. However, that is that equivalent of saying that the relation between dollars and students trained is $Y = \$889(Z^1)$ (see row 2 of Table 2), a linear regression equation which assumes that each incremental student produces $889 worth of satisfaction to society. If we prefer to think in terms of thousand-dollar units for simplicity, then the regression equation becomes $Y = .89(X)$ (see row 1 of Table 2). However, this linearity is contrary to our expectation that added training will have diminishing returns. If these are medical students, a society or a community would obtain more benefit from the first student trained than from the one-hundredth student trained after it already has ninety-nine.

What is therefore needed is a way of converting the turning-point equation of $4,000 = 4.5$ students into an equation that shows reasonable diminishing returns. A simple and meaningful way of doing this is to divide the logarithm of $4 by the logarithm of 4.5 students. (A logarithm is an exponent to which ten or another number is raised in order to equal a given number.) That quotient then becomes the exponent in a nonlinear regression equation of the form $Y = a(X)^b$, where $a = 1$. With these factors, the equation is $Y = (X)^{.92}$, because log 4/log 4.5 = .60/.65 = .92 (see row 3 of Table 2). These calculations are easy to make on a hand calculator that is capable of determining logarithms. Here is one proof that the translation equation makes

Table 2. Deriving the Translation Equation from the Turning-Point Equation, the Method of Curve Fitting, and the Monetary Units

Inputs			Outputs	
Turning-Point Equation (Dollars to Students)	Method of Curve Fitting	Monetary Units	Slope (Dollars to Students)	Translation Equation (Dollars to Students)
(1) $4=4.5	Linear	$1,000	4.5/4	$Y=.89(X)$
(2) $4,000=4.5	Linear	$1	4,000/4.5	$Y=889(X)$
(3) $4=4.5	Double-log	$1,000	log 4/log 4.5	$Y=(X)^{.92}$
(4) $4,000=4.5	Double-log	$1,000	log 4,000/log 4.5	$Y=(X)^{5.51}$
(5) $4=4.5	Semilog	$1,000	4/log 4.5	$Y=6.12 \log X$
(6) $4,000=4.5	Semilog	$1	4,000/log 4.5	$Y=6124 \log X$
(7) $1=4.5	Double-log	$4,000	log 1/log 4.5	$Y=(X)^0=1$
(8) $4.5=4.5	Double-log	$889	log 4.5/log 4.5	$Y=(X)^1=X$
(9) $4,000=1	Double-log	$1	log 4,000/log 1	undefined
(10) $.50=4.5	Double-log	$8,000	log .50/log 4.5	$Y=(X)^{-.46}$
(11) $4=.50	Double-log	$.11	log 4/log .50	$Y=(X)^{-2.00}$

sense: Replace X in the equation with 4.5, raise it to the power .92, and observe that the resulting Y is $4. Likewise, if we replace X in the equation with 0, the resulting Y is 0, which also makes sense. It can be shown that the nonlinear equation $Y = a(X)^b$ is the equivalent of the logarithmic-linear equation $\log Y = \log a + b \log X$ by the following steps: Take the log of both sides of the nonlinear equation. The result is $\log Y = \log(aX^b)$. Simplify that equation. The result is $\log Y = \log a + \log(X^b)$. That equation further simplifies to $\log Y = \log a + b \log X$, which is the logarithmic-linear equation. Solving for b in that equation yields $b = (\log Y - \log a)/\log X$. When log X equals zero, then log Y equals zero. This means that, when X equals one, Y equals one, and the a in $Y = aX^b$ equals one. Finally, if a equals one, then $\log a$ equals zero, and the equation $b = (\log Y - \log a)/\log X$ simplifies to $b = \log Y/\log X$.

We can now compare policy A with policy B to see which generates more monetary value. Policy A generates a monetary value of $Y = (30)^{.92}$ or $22.85 (that is, 22.85 monetary units of $22,850) for students trained. Policy A generates a monetary value of $Y = (10)^{.90}$ or $7.95 for patients treated. The total for policy A is $30.79. Policy B generates a monetary value of $Y = (20)^{.92}$ or $15.74 for students trained and a monetary value of $Y = (18)^{.90}$ or $13.48 for patients treated. The total for policy B is $29.22. Policy A thus generates more monetary value than policy B. The key subjective element in this analysis is where the turning-point or threshold equation is. The paired-comparison monetizing method tends to consider all the values of the relevant decision makers, although it does not disaggregate their values into separate components. Many people are comfortable working with monetized values. Paired-comparison monetizing reduces the value judgment to one of determining the point at which a set of nonmonetary benefits is equal to a given number of dollars. This example is summarized in Table 1, where the policies are referred to as X's, the intermediate goal scores are referred to as Z's, and the more nearly ultimate goals of maximizing monetary gain is referred to as Y. For nonlinear logarithmic curve-fitting, the reader can consult Draper and Smith (1966), Cohen and Cohen (1975), and Hilton (1976).

Instead of using the division-of-logarithms approach to arrive at the .92 exponent, we can use a hand calculator that is capable of linear regression analysis. Performing the calculation involves inputting the X value of log 4.5, the Y value of log 4, the X value of log 1, and the Y value of log 1. Pressing the b or slope button causes the calculator to display .92. By pressing the a or intercept button, one can cause the calculator to display a zero. That number needs to be unlogged to become meaningful. To unlog it, press the button labeled *10^x*. A one will then appear on the display. One is the value of the scale coefficient or the multiplier in the equation $Y = a(x)^b$. It is not important in this context, since any number multiplied by one remains the same number.

If one presses the r button, a one will appear on the display. The one indicates that two data points have been inserted into the calculator and that they are both on the regression curve, which means a perfect correlation. The correlation is always perfect when there are only two data points. Normally, two is too small a sample for generalization to a large population or universe of data points. In this context, however, if we consider the data point of $4 and 4.5 students as reflecting the values of the relevant decision maker or makers accurately, no sampling is being done. Where there is more than one key decision maker, then each pair of interpolated threshold scores can be inserted as a separate data point. However, it is easier to average those scores and use the resulting average as the key data point. The other data point of zero dollars and zero students trained is an assumed data point reflecting the reasonable assumption that training no students generates no dollar values.

Variations on the Basic Ideas

One variation on the basic idea is to use a semilog rather than a double-log regression analysis for converting the turning-point equation into a diminishing-returns equation. The double-log analysis involves a logarithmic transformation of both the nonmonetary benefits and the dollar amount at the turning point. By logging both the input and the output variables, we obtain numerical parameters for an equation of the form $\log y = \log a + b \log X$. This equation is algebraically equivalent to $Y = a(X)^b$ if one takes the log of both sides of this equation. The semilog approach is simpler but less meaningful. It involves logging only the input variable. The general form is $Y = a + b \log X$. For the turning-point equation of $4,000 = 4.5 students, this means that the calculator works with a first data point whose coordinates are the logs of 4.5 and 4 and a second data point whose coordinates are the logs of one and zero. If we input these data into the statistical calculator, 6.12 is displayed when we press the b button and zero when we press the a button. These two numbers inform us that the semilog translation equation is $Y = 6.12 \log X$. This equation fits the data in the sense that the log of 4.5 is .65 and that .65 multiplied by 6.12 equals four monetary units (see row 5 of Table 2).

The semilog approach has two big disadvantages: The 6.12 does not have a simple interpretation, and it results in diminishing returns that tend to diminish more sharply than seems consistent with common sense. The small b or elasticity coefficient in a double-log equation shows the percentage change that occurs in Y when X undergoes a 1 percent increase. In other words, the percentage change in the relation between Y and X is constant, although the absolute change is a curve. The small b or regression coefficient in a semilog equation shows the percentage change that occurs in Y when X undergoes a change of ten absolute units — a complex construction for purposes of interpretation. More important, X has to increase by very large quantities in order to show much change in Y, because the returns tend to diminish sharply, not smoothly as they do in the double-log equation.

The big advantage of the semilog approach is that a semilog fit will guarantee diminishing returns regardless of the nonmonetary benefits and the dollar value. This is not so with the double-log approach. To guarantee diminishing, rather than increasing or constant, returns with the double-log fit, we have to transform the numbers in the turning-point equation so that the numerical value of the nonmonetary benefits is greater than the numerical value of the dollar amount. For example, if we had inputted the numbers 4,000 and 4.5 into the calculator instead of 4 and 4.5, then we would have a double-log equation equal to $Y = (X)^{5.51}$ (see row 4 of Table 2). That equation shows returns increasing rather than diminishing. This means that, if X increases from 1 to 2, Y increases from 1 to a number much larger than 2. With the double-log equation of $Y = (X)^{.92}$, when X increases from 1 to 2, Y increases from 1 to a number smaller than 2.

If we work with the numbers 4,000 and 4.5 instead of with 4 and 4.5, and we use the semilog approach, then we obtain the semilog equation $Y = 7,124 \log X$. This equation will generate diminishing returns in the sense that, when we go from an X value of 1 to 2, we go from a Y value of 0 to 1,844, but when we go from an X value of 9 to 10, we go from a Y value of 5,818 to 6,124, a much smaller increment than 1,884 (see row 6 of Table 2).

The legitimate way of causing the numerical value of the nonmonetary benefits to be greater than the numerical value of the dollar amount is to express the dollar amount in thousands or millions of dollars by dividing the dollar amount by 1,000 or 1,000,000. Doing so does not change the turning-point equation; it changes only the scale or units of measurement. Nothing is distorted, just so long as one translates back by multiplying the result by 1,000 or 1,000,000.

In converting the dollar amount into a number of monetary units that is smaller than the number of nonmonetary benefits, one cannot divide by the dollar amount. Thus, if the dollar amount is $4,000, we cannot divide by 4,000 and obtain one monetary unit. Doing so would result in the double-log equation $Y = 1(X)^0 = 1$, because the log of 1 is 0, which is the numerator of the exponent (see row 7 of Table 2). Likewise, the system cannot work with a turning-point equation in which the nonmonetary benefits (the numerator) equal the dollar amount (the denominator). Doing so would result in the double-log equation $Y = 1(X)^1 = X$ (see row 8 of Table 2). If the turning-point equation involves a dollar amount equal to one nonmonetary unit, then the slope, exponent, or elasticity coefficient involves dividing by zero, which is mathematically undefined (see row 9 of Table 2).

Although we cannot divide $4,000 by 4,000 or by 889 where there are 4.5 students in the turning-point equation, we can divide $4,000 by any other number larger than 889 (or $Y/$X) and still generate the equivalent of the same diminishing-returns translation equation. For example, we can divide $4,000 by 8,000 and talk of a turning-point equation where ½ or .5 of a monetary unit equals 4.5 nonmonetary benefits. Inputting that information into the statistical calculator yields the double-log equation $Y = (X)^{-.46}$, since the log of .50 divided by the log of 4.5 is − .46 (see row 10 of Table 2). That relation is unacceptable, since it shows a negative relation between dollars and students trained, which implies that training more students lowers satisfaction as measured in dollars. Likewise, the turning-point equation expressed in row 11 is unacceptable because the nonmonetary benefit units are expressed as being less than one. The log of a number less than one is negative, and the resulting elasticity coefficient is negative. If both the dollar amount and the nonmonetary benefits are negative (smaller than one), then dividing the one by the other will give a positive elasticity coefficient.

This analysis indicates that many equations are the equivalent of $Y = (X)^{.92}$ depending on the monetary units used. However, the equation that we have been using is the most convenient, since thousand-dollar units are easy to handle. The dollar amount must be less than the nonmonetary benefits if we are to prevent increasing returns or constant returns, and neither should be one. That requirement is easy to meet, because we can change the monetary units by dividing the dollar amount by a convenient large number. The relations between the translation equation, the turning-point equation, and the method of curve fitting are summarized in Table 2. The meaningfulness of each equation can be proved by replacing X with 4.5, doing the arithmetic, and observing that the value of Y is whatever appears in the turning-point equation. Tufte (1974), Lewis (1966), and Guilford (1954) compare double-log and semilog curve fitting.

Another variation on the basic idea of transforming a paired-comparison turning-point equation into a diminishing-returns translation equation relates to nonmonetary goals that are detriments, not benefits. A good example is crime. One can ask a series of paired-comparison questions in order to arrive at a turning-point equation of the form $8,000 = 12 burglaries or 8 monetary units = 12 burglaries. However, it would be meaningless to divide 8 by 12 or the log of 8 by the log of 12 in order to arrive at a linear slope or a nonlinear elasticity coefficient, because dividing dollars by nonmonetary benefits makes sense only when the denominator is a benefit. A burglary is not a benefit like a student trained or a patient treated. Training no students generates no dollar value. In contrast, having no burglaries may be quite valuable in a big city. The relation between dollars and students trained is a positively sloping diminishing-returns curve in which $$Y$ equals zero when X equals zero. The relation between dollars and burglaries is a negatively sloping diminishing-returns curve in which $$Y$ may be quite high when X equals zero, but we have no way of knowing the value of Y when X equals zero.

The best way of handling the monetizing of detriments like burglaries (as contrasted with benefits like students trained) is to convert the detriments into a benefit. This is often easy to do. For example, an unemployment rate of 10 percent can be converted into an employment rate of 90 percent. Where there is no meaningful 100 percent or other number from which to subtract, we can try to talk in terms of detriments reduced, whether the detriments in question are burglaries, cancer deaths, or automobile accidents. Doing so here would yield a turning-point equation of the form $8,000 = 12$ burglaries reduced. By changing the wording of the nonmonetary goal, we can now handle it as a nonmonetary benefit and subject it to monetizing by using paired comparisons and the double-log transformation method for showing diminishing positive returns.

Some Conclusions

The following conclusions concerning the handling of nonmonetary benefits and multidimensional trade-offs can be drawn from the preceding analysis.

Incremental analysis, which involves working with the raw scores in their original dimensions, is the simplest approach to use from the perspective of the policy evaluator and the decision maker. However, the method is difficult to work with when there are many policies or many goals. Working with many policies requires comparing them two at a time. If there are N policies, there must be $N-1$ paired comparisons. The policy that remains after $N-1$ comparisons is the winner. Working with many goals means expressing the preference question in a form like this: Which is better to have, an extra seventeen B_1 units and an extra five B_4 units, or an extra nine B^2 units and an extra twelve B_3 units? The process gets a bit clumsy with multiple goals and multiple policies.

The percentaging method can easily handle multiple policies, since it does not require paired comparisons of the alternatives. The percentaging method can also handle multiple goals, although each goal has to be assigned a relative weight. The best way of doing this is generally to assign the least important goal a weight of one and to express the weights for the other goals in terms of how many more times they are valued than the least important goal. The results enable one to arrive at a best policy or combination of policies in light of the goals, their weights, the policies, and their scores on the goals. However, the bottom-line scores are expressed in percentages, and most people feel more comfortable with dollars than they do with percentages. One may also find it difficult to arrive at multiple weights where there are multiple goals. Percentaging is also not meaningful if the relations between policies and goals cannot be quantified, whereas incremental analysis can handle nonquantitative relations.

Although incremental analysis and percentaging analysis may be preferable for the reasons given, if the analyst prefers to monetize nonmonetary benefits, then the method of paired comparisons presented in this chapter may be more meaningful than the method of shadow prices, which attempts to think of nonmonetary benefits in terms of market values. Market-oriented analysis tends to overemphasize values that have relatively close market analogues; it tends to overemphasize the values of the marketplace and to discount the values of decision makers or stakeholders. The paired-comparisons method tends to consider all the values, although it does not disaggregate them into their separate components. It especially considers the values of the decision makers, since they are the ones to whom the paired-comparison questions are put. The system is fairly simple to apply both at the questioning stage and at the second stage, where the turning-point data are put into a regression analysis to obtain a diminishing-returns equation that translates nonmonetary benefits into dollars.

It must be recognized that accurately monetizing all the nonmonetary benefits will not necessarily enable one to arrive at an optimum policy. (The author thanks Michael Birnbaum of the University of Illinois psychology department for pointing out that accurately monetizing all the benefits and costs in a policy evaluation will not necessarily result in choosing the best policy, in view of the relations between monetizing and satisfaction units.) The maximizing of satisfaction may conflict with the maximizing of dollar returns, even if one accepts that there is a positive relation between satisfaction and dollars, so long as one also accepts that there is a diminishing-returns relation. That paradox can be dealt with by noting whether one is dealing with a situation where a reasonable transformation can make a difference, which sometimes occurs. In these unusual situations, the use of the concept of threshold transformation can be helpful in deciding whether the rank order of the leading policies needs to be reversed.

All three methods for dealing with nonmonetary benefits are relatively new in the field of benefit-cost analysis, although the field as a whole is fairly new. All three methods have both technical aspects and commonsense aspects, but with more emphasis on the simplicity and face validity of common sense. All three methods are subject to further analysis and to further improvement. It is hoped that this chapter will stimulate further thinking about methods of dealing with nonmonetary benefits in public-sector benefit-cost analysis, where nonmonetary benefits are so prevalent. Doing so may help to clarify the meaningfulness of allocation theory in political science with regard to who gets and who should get what, when, how, and why. When benefits and costs have been monetized, one can input the monetized benefits and costs into optimizing models in order to arrive at an optimum choice, risk, level, or mix. Such models are discussed by White and others (1980), Stokey and Zeckhauser (1978), and Nagel (1982).

References

Baumol, W. *Economic Theory and Operations Analysis*. Englewood Cliffs, N.J.: Prentice-Hall, 1977.
Bui, X. T. *Executive Planning with BASIC*. Berkeley, Calif.: Sybex, 1981.
Chase, S. (Ed.). *Problems in Public Expenditure Analysis*. Washington, D.C.: Brookings Institution, 1968.
Cohen, J., and Cohen, P. *Applied Regression Analysis*. New York: Wiley, 1975.
Draper, N. R., and Smith, H. *Applied Regression Analysis*. New York: Wiley, 1966.

Edwards, W., and Newman, R. *Multiattribute Evaluation.* Beverly Hills, Calif.: Sage, 1982.
Gramlich, E. *Benefit-Cost Analysis of Government Programs.* Englewood Cliffs, N.J.: Prentice-Hall, 1981.
Grether, D., and Wilde, L. "An Analysis of Conjunctive Choice: Theory and Experiments." *Journal of Consumer Research,* 1974, *10,* 373–385.
Guilford, J. P. *Psychometric Methods.* New York: McGraw-Hill, 1954.
Henerson, M., and others. *How to Measure Attitudes.* Beverly Hills, Calif.: Sage, 1978.
Hilton, G. *Intermediate Politometrics.* New York: Columbia University Press, 1976.
Keeney, R., and Raiffa, H. *Decisions with Multiple Objectives: Preferences and Value Tradeoffs.* New York: Wiley, 1976.
Lewis, D. *Quantitative Methods in Psychology.* Iowa City: University of Iowa Press, 1966.
Mishan, E. *Cost-Benefit Analysis.* New York: Praeger, 1976.
Nagel, S. *Policy Evaluation: Making Optimum Decisions.* New York: Praeger, 1982.
Nagel, S. "Nonmonetary Variables in Benefit-Cost Analysis." *Evaluation Review,* 1983a, *7,* 37–64.
Nagel, S. *Public Policy: Goals, Means, and Methods.* New York: St. Martin's Press, 1983b.
Nagel, S. "Unknown Variables in Policy/Program Evaluation." *Evaluation and Program Planning,* 1983c, *6,* 7–18.
Phillips, L., and Votey, H. *The Economics of Crime Control.* Beverly Hills, Calif.: Sage, 1981.
Rhoads, S. (Ed.). *Valuing Life: Public Policy Dilemmas.* Denver: Westview Press, 1980.
Rose, A., and Prell, A. "Does the Punishment Fit the Crime? A Study in Social Valuation." *American Journal of Sociology,* 1955, *61,* 247–254.
Saaty, T. *Analytic Hierarchy Process: Planning, Priority Setting, Resource Allocation.* New York: McGraw-Hill, 1980.
Sellin, T., and Wolfgang, M. *The Measurement of Delinquency.* New York: Wiley, 1964.
Stokey, E., and Zeckhauser, R. *A Primer for Policy Analysis.* New York: Norton, 1978.
Sugden, R., and Williams, A. *The Principles of Practical Cost-Benefit Analysis.* London: Oxford University Press, 1978.
Thompson, M. *Benefit-Cost Analysis for Program Evaluation.* Beverly Hills, Calif.: Sage, 1980.
Tufte, E. *Data Analysis for Politics and Policy.* Englewood Cliffs, N.J.: Prentice-Hall, 1974.
White, M., and others. *Managing Public Systems: Analytic Techniques for Public Administration.* North Scituate, Mass.: Duxbury, 1980.
Zeleny, M. *Multiple Criteria Decision Making.* New York: McGraw-Hill, 1982.

Stuart S. Nagel is professor of political science, University of Illinois, Champaign.

Capital costs are substantial, frequently problematical, and often neglected or inappropriately estimated in deliberations over how to deliver public services, such as mental health care.

Capital Costs in Economic Program Evaluation: The Case of Mental Health Services

Nancy L. Cannon, Thomas McGuire Barbara Dickey

Evaluation of the relative economic efficiency of various mental health treatment alternatives is a popular focus for mental health researchers today. Which programs prove to achieve their goals at the lowest cost is of increasing interest. The clinical effectiveness of lower-intensity care, such as alternatives to hospitalization, or short length of stay has been established in the recent literature (Mosher, 1983). Attention is turning to the implied cost savings of substitutes for hospital stays. Entering the world of cost analysis raises several major hurdles for the mental health researcher. For instance, a review of the literature reveals problems associated with the need for distinguishing social cost from budget cost (McGuire and Dickey, 1983), the tendency to accept charges as a proxy for social cost and the bias thus introduced (Finkler, 1982), and failure to include important cost components in the cost model (Rubin, 1980). Capital cost presents an overarching problem when the cost analysis involves public facilities. The capital portion of the ledger potentially dominates the total; publicly owned capital is not valued by the market, and the researcher is presented with a special set of problems.

To test an approach to market valuation of public property, we performed a case study at an urban Boston mental health facility. We encountered several problems in observing the market price of the site, and these problems guided the development of the valuation procedure. This chapter has three purposes: first, to review past treatments of capital cost in mental health research; second, to outline methods of valuing publicly owned capital based on opportunity cost; third, to test this approach in a case study.

Accounting Versus Economic Cost

In analyses of general hospital costs, capital cost has typically been handled in a variety of ways, although there has been some effort at standardization. These ways range from a strict accountancy approach, in which a depreciation figure is used to account for the assets shown on the facility's balance sheet (Long, 1980), to the use of elaborate financial analysis models designed to capture the true value of capital for the firm (Vraciw, 1980). When budgetary or cost accounting data are used as the basis for depicting the cost components of treatment, other social costs remain unidentified. Since a comprehensive cost comparison includes all costs to society (that is, the economic costs of the treatment options), the opportunity cost of capital is an important element of such an analysis.

For purposes of cost-benefit and cost-effectiveness studies in mental health, researchers have frequently accepted the per diem charge or a total cost per person rate developed by the organization's accountants as a reflection of the cost of treatment in that setting. To arrive at this figure, retrospective annual costs for all inputs associated with a specific form of treatment are retrieved (usually disaggregated only to the departmental level). The composite amount is then divided by the units of service multiplied by time. That is,

$$\frac{TC}{N \times T}$$

where TC is total cost, N is the number of patients served, and T is units of time, such as 365 days. Typically, a per diem includes a depreciation figure as well as interest costs associated with loan repayment. This rate is a unit of measure common to both private and public mental health care settings. Its use assumes that long-run average cost is equal to price; that is, the per diem rate is a substitute for the market price charged to payers. Since long-run average cost equals price in a competitive market, a per diem that accounts for three components—depreciation, operating costs, and debt service (that is, rate of return)—should equal cost.

In using an organization's per diem rate, mental health care researchers may restrict themselves in identifying true costs associated with different modes of treatment. For example, May (1971) sought to identify treatment cost differences for groups of randomly assigned patients in a mental health setting. May noted that it was difficult to go beyond the hospital's established per diem rate. Thus, not only was May's research effort constrained in its ability to model the costs related to each form of therapy, it was also unable, due to the aggregation of resources under general department headings, to ascertain the specific inputs assigned to various therapeutic models.

Subsequently, Cassell and others (1972) attempted to compare the cost of pre- and post discharge services for more than 400 discharged patients. Use of per diem rates for estimating the pre-discharge costs resulted in a wide range of patient costs, ranging from a high of $30,000 to a low of $7,000, and it precluded the specification of different combinations of resources that created the observed disparity in total cost per patient. This study highlights the problem of heterogeneity, which is masked by per diem rates. Generally, only one inpatient rate is used, regardless of the treatment or of differences in service intensity among the patients.

Several other research efforts accepted per diem rates as an element of cost analysis, and the literature pays careful attention to some of the other potential drawbacks to their use (Sorensen and Kucic, 1981; Zelman and others, 1982). The assumption that long-run average cost is revealed in a per diem (average) rate, one element of which is capital, is key to this discussion. The researcher who accepts this rate has introduced an inaccurate cost estimate, in that it ignores the organization's method of recording capital cost. Moreover, it has been our experience that public hospitals sometimes fail to record any capital cost, since the facility may have long since been depreciated.

In other words, the value of capital should be a factor in cost evaluation, but the assumptions implicit in per diem rates may be inadequate or invalid. For instance, in a competitive market, price may not reflect long-run average cost. Similarly, in a market where the buyer is a monopsonist (as may be the case with state purchasers of mental health care), price may be below long-run average cost. Depreciation is one important component of the per diem rate. In most facilities, it is an arbitrary rate, and as such it may create error. The problem is pervasive. There is a pattern of artificiality in the formulation of depreciation factors for hospitals, particularly for nonprofit institutions. Moreover, in the majority of public facilities, the problem is compounded by an absence of debt service. (While government entities repay their loans, the repayment is not tied to specific facilities.) Finally, there is no resale of public facilities that allows us to value capital periodically.

The Mendota Cost-Benefit Study

Recently, efforts have been made to improve the overall estimation of costs associated with mental health treatment. Some studies have included explication of the cost of public facilities. At the Mendota Mental Health Institute in Madison, Wisconsin, Weisbrod and others (1980) sought to develop a comprehensive model for estimating the cost of alternative treatments in two types of settings.

Weisbrod and colleagues applied an economic approach to cost determination. In handling the costs associated with inpatient care, the components of the institute's per diem rate were first reviewed. The rate was then corrected to reflect the decrease when all research costs were removed and the increase when the cost of capital was included. Ignoring accounting entries for depreciation expense, the researchers substituted an estimate of the market rate of return from which a single value for the user cost of capital was derived. Because the Mendota Institute is a public facility, there was no market rental rate. It was therefore necessary to estimate the stock value of the facility (that is, the current market price) and use this estimate to derive a flow or rental value that could be included in the analysis.

The authors indicate that "the per diem cost estimate was adjusted upward to allow for an opportunity cost of 8 percent on the estimated value of the land and for the depreciated replacement cost of the physical plant" (Weisbrod and others, 1980, p. 402). Elsewhere, Weisbrod (1983, p. 820) noted that he had used "a 9 percent rate of return on the market value of that portion of the hospital plant and land that was used in the treatment of the inpatient group." Weisbrod's use of this rate of return and the steps used to obtain a market value and a replacement cost for the Mendota Mental Health Institute were not fully detailed. (For example, it is not clear what cost base was used to estimate the stock value of the plant. One procedure would take booked value of land and buildings, based on historical cost, as depreciation basis. Another procedure would use a replacement cost figure or current market value.) Nonetheless, the impact of the adjustment on the per diem rate was unmistakable: The daily rate for treatment on the inpatient side increased from $70 to $100.

In general, the Mendota study set a new standard for cost analysis in mental health in that it fully explicated a variety of cost variables that had previously gone unspecified. The methodology developed for deriving shadow prices for unpriced resources has enhanced the ability of researchers to assess trade-offs among different mental health treatment models produced in the public sector. However, the study's approach to the valuation of capital requires refinement.

The study essentially described all costs associated with two distinct modes of treatment for severely disturbed patients: One was based in the institution, and the other was a community-based alternative. After deriving a per patient cost for the two program options, the authors were able to demonstrate that the benefits of the community-based model of care outweighed the costs. The community services benefit-cost ratio was higher than the corresponding ratio for the inpatient treatment model.

The importance of the role of capital is striking in that the findings of Weisbrod and colleagues on the institution side were so sensitive to the rental price derived for the plant itself. Either a small change in the rate of return used or use of a more modest replacement cost estimate would bring the benefit-cost outcome for the institutional treatment program into line with that for the community model. For example, in a hypothetical modeling of the capital cost estimate for the Mendota Institute, the average cost per patient for the inpatient treatment program was adjusted downward by $140 when the rate of return was lowered to 4 percent. Use of this lower rate, the sum of a return on capital and depreciation, is justified in light of experience in capital markets over the last several years. Revising the rate had the effect of reducing the benefit-cost differential between the two comparison programs by 40 percent.

Admittedly, this exercise involved the use of several assumptions, of which one was that the replacement cost used was in the high range. Put another way, the 1973 replacement cost for the Mendota Institute appears to have been an upper bound on possible cost estimates for deriving a capital value. Had a more modest cost estimate been used, the impact of the capital cost on the inpatient per diem would have been substantially less than the $30 reported in the study. Clearly, inclusion of capital cost in the Mendota study had salutary effects. Our intention here has been to demonstrate possibilities for further work in the estimation of parameters for this cost component. The discussion that follows is designed to illustrate the principles underlying measurement of capital cost and to outline a model for developing more robust cost estimates. Then, to highlight the problems related to this aspect of cost estimation and to illustrate some possible solutions, we present relevant data and findings from a recently completed mental health cost-effectiveness study.

Methods for Measuring Capital Costs

The problem for researchers is to make the best use of available data concerning a capital facility and to extract the economic cost of use of that facility for mental health treatment programs. Ideally, the researcher would observe the rental price that the market would be willing to pay for the facility over a period of time, such as a year. This rental price is the value that the highest bidder would place on use of the facility. This value is referred to as *opportunity cost*. Note that opportunity cost is determined by the value of the facility to potential users. It may be greater or less than the annualized value of the reproduction cost of the facility. If the facility were produced and sold in competitive markets, a demand price (opportunity cost) above replacement cost would signal to builders that they could construct similar facilities at a profit. If the demand price fell short of construction costs, no similar facilities could be produced and cover costs, and no net construction would take place. Thus, in the long run, when markets are in equilibrium, demand price tends to equal replacement cost.

In the public sector, construction decisions are not determined by anticipated profits or losses, and the connection between value in alternative use and replacement cost is further weakened. Since public facilities serving the mentally ill are not often rented on the open market, neither the replacement cost nor market rent, the flow and stock measures of opportunity cost, are usually accessible to researchers. Thus to piece together a sensible estimate of capital costs, it is helpful to start by understanding the relationships among the costs associated with capital. Figure 1 shows how markets determine the opportunity cost of a facility and the relationship between the opportunity cost measured in flow terms (a rental) and in stock terms (a capital value). The explanation that follows applies to a single existing facility.

Demand and supply in local rental markets set the gross rent for space of comparable quality in the area. Operating costs play no part in the setting of market rent; the market price is determined by outside forces. Market rent is one measure of the facility's opportunity cost. Market rent is equal to the value that the market (that is, renters) place on space of comparable quality. As we proceed with our explanation of Figure 1, we will see how rental value first covers cost and provides the building owners with the competitive rate of return on capital.

The owners of the facility must pay expenses, including operating costs and depreciation, from gross rent. The magnitude of these expenses is strongly influenced by their tax treatment, which will be ignored in this discussion. Deduction of expenses leaves the owner with net rent. It is net rent, along with the competitive rate of return on assets of similar risk, that determines the capital value of the facility. If N is the net rent and r is the rate of return on similar assets, the value of the facility, V, is given by the equation

$$V = \frac{N}{r}$$

Figure 1. Relationship Between the Stock and Flow Measures of Capital Cost

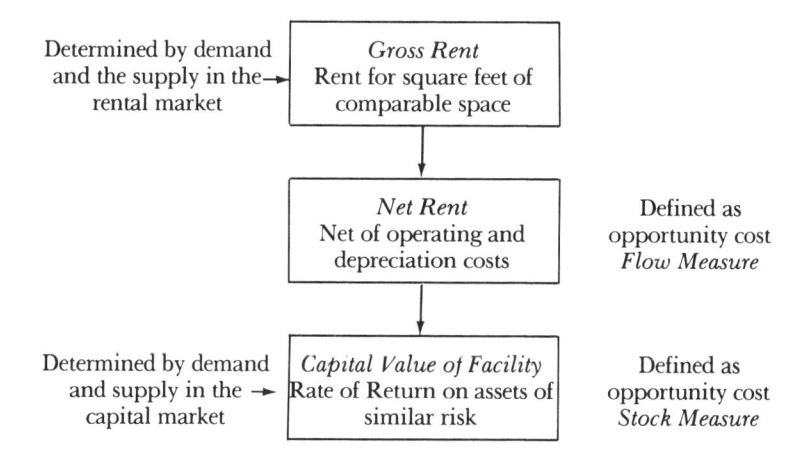

Determined by demand and the supply in the rental market →	**Gross Rent** Rent for square feet of comparable space	
	↓	
	Net Rent Net of operating and depreciation costs	Defined as opportunity cost *Flow Measure*
	↓	
Determined by demand and supply in the → capital market	*Capital Value of Facility* Rate of Return on assets of similar risk	Defined as opportunity cost *Stock Measure*

In other words, the market value of the building is equal to the amount that would make the net rent equal to the competitive rate of return. It is the net rent that determines the capital value of the building, not the other way around. The capital value of the facility—what it would sell for on a competitive market—may be greater or less than the replacement cost, as already noted.

The market value of the facility is the second stock measure of the opportunity cost of the facility. It can be converted into the market rental or flow value by retracing the steps by which the facility is valued by the market. Given the capital value of the facility, equation 1 can be rewritten to solve for the net rent. (This is not the causal flow of the relation, but it is true nonetheless.) Next, estimates of opportunity cost and depreciation can be added in order to estimate gross market rent.

Although in principle these two methods would lead to a similar result, direct observation of gross rent is clearly the preferred approach. Estimations of capital value, rate of return, depreciation (as distorted by taxes), and operating costs all involve considerable error. The resulting estimate of gross rent is thus highly subject to error. Nevertheless, this procedure is often the only choice available when the focus is public mental health facilities. To test the model, we performed a case study. The next section details the process we used and its outcome.

From Principle to Application: A Case Study

In 1979, researchers at Boston's Massachusetts Mental Health Center (MMHC) launched a clinical study that built on earlier treatment outcome studies of the chronically mentally ill. The controlled experiment, conducted over a two-year period, was designed to produce empirical evidence of significant differences in patient outcomes for those receiving conventional inpatient treatment and those participating in an innovative psychosocial program. Both treatment programs were provided within the public hospital setting. A carefully constructed research design and use of multiple outcome measures were strong points in the original clinical study. Because data on services delivered were collected at the level of individual patients, it was possible to perform a cost-effectiveness analysis of the alternative treatment models.

Following Weisbrod's lead, we developed a cost model that specified all economic factors associated with patient care and delivery of the two modes of treatment. One of the most significant cost categories was the cost of capital related to the public facility, the Massachusetts Mental Health Center. Before applying the market valuation model to MMHC, we formulated several descriptors for the site. The usefulness of competitive market assumptions was then tested. Construction of a range of rental rates for use in the cost analysis was the final step.

The Site. The cost-effectiveness study was conducted at a large urban mental health center located in Boston. It is the primary public mental health service setting for 200,000 people in its economically and racially mixed catchment area. It is also a teaching hospital for Harvard Medical School, and it conducts research that is funded by a variety of public and private sources. The mental health center is supported primarily by the state legislature, which mandates budget appropriations to specific hospitals through the Department of Mental Health. During the study period, 1979–1981, the facility had ninety inpatient beds and a large outpatient department.

The center's property spans 113,000 square feet; more than 45,000 square feet are covered with buildings, some dating back to 1907. It is positioned in an area that has emerged as the Boston medical services area, and as such it is easily recognizable as prime commercial real estate in the current Boston market.

The Valuation Procedure. As described in the preceding discussion of market valuation assumptions, observed market rental rates provide the preferred mechanism for estimation of capital value. Attempts were made to identify comparable market rents (for example, for nearby professional office space and so forth). The research team experienced difficulty, however, since local buildings are predominantly held by trusts. The validity of rents was not clear, in that in several instances the owners (hospitals) leased from themselves. However, we obtained the rental rate for a neighboring parking garage, and we used that figure later as a point of comparison in calculating opportunity cost for the MMHC facility.

Since rental rates for the MMHC or for comparables were not available, it was necessary to establish a stock measure for the property and plant; this value would then be converted into a flow measure. Before collecting data, we assessed the impact of the MMHC's location on the generalizability or representativeness of study findings. It could be argued that establishment of a market price for the 2.6-acre site is complicated by the fact that the MMHC is located within the borders of Boston's medical mile. In a sense, it was serendipity that this aging hospital was now located in a high-rent district, a circumstance that makes its site somewhat unusual. However, the valuation of any public hospital facility would require interpolation of information unique to the particular site. The research team chose to describe the forces observed in the market for the MMHC and used these to outline general procedures for analyzing the findings in such a case.

While it was a simple matter to determine the need for a value of the opportunity cost of capital in this case, it was quite difficult to estimate the magnitude of the task. Clearly, the principle of value determination—willingness to pay—applied. The problem lay in operationalization of the principle. With no explicit market price to guide the process, the research team outlined three options for use in estimating a stock value: First, conduct a survey of willingness to pay among affected or interested parties and hope that true preferences would be revealed or that the exaggerations would cancel out the understatements. Second, obtain documentation for real estate transactions revealing market price for comparable property in the area. Third, to estimate willingness to pay, compute the cost of replacement. This will be neither an upper or a lower bound, with the absence of market forces determining public construction. No single choice was satisfactory. The key problem associated with each option is summarized in Figure 2.

The research team acknowledged but disregarded two other possibilities. All other social costs (for the larger study) could be computed to yield a net social cost for each program exclusive of the value of capital. Thus, if the cost of one program is already substantially lower than the alternative, the program is definitely more efficient, and an exact calculation of the cost of capital need not be attempted. Or, as a last resort, only a qualitative description of the impact of the cost of capital on overall program costs might be developed. The last option effectively shifts the burden of analysis to the public decision maker.

Valuation of the MMHC facility required a combination of the tasks outlined in Figure 2. First, the concerned actors were surveyed; in some cases, written records were used as an expression of willingness to pay. (It was hoped that individuals and institutional representatives would reveal true preferences.) In addition, an analogue was sought in private market activity. Where local property of comparable use and real estate characteristics had been traded, its price was used as a guide to the value of the MMHC parcel. Estimates of replacement cost were also obtained.

Market Characteristics. In the part of Boston where the MMHC is located, surrounding hospitals are reportedly seeking opportunities for expansion, and several are in the middle of major capital construction projects. It was assumed, therefore, that hospitals with property adjacent to the MMHC within a two-block radius were potential buyers. It was also assumed that the property had other uses. A consulting commercial developer proposed that the highest private demand for the site would be for professional office uses. Public demand included a preference for maintaining the current use of the site or alternatively for making it available for other public operations (that is, for use in delivery of other human services or criminal justice services).

Estimates of Market Price. Complications introduced by virtue of the

Figure 2. Operational Alternatives: Cost Estimation

Option	Problem
Survey interested actors	Difficult to observe willingness to pay
Document market price of comparables	May be unavailable
Derive the replacement cost	Replacement cost may be unrelated to current market value

variety of potential buyers were compounded by the fact that everyone involved in valuing the property faced different, perhaps conflicting, incentives when it came to estimating the value of the property. The price information came from four distinct sources; a summary of the collection process and its outcome appears in Table 1.

The cost data included the purchase price of a parcel located around the block from MMHC property that was considered to be of comparable value; the adjusted historical cost estimate used in development of the facility's current depreciation schedule by an appraisal consultant to the state; a 1984 estimate constructed by an expert witness, in this case a highly recommended commercial realtor-developer who once headed Boston's redevelopment agency; and the replacement cost estimate submitted by a Boston architectual and development firm in 1980.

Table 1 shows the estimates, their sources, and the period in which they were made. All prices were deflated (or inflated) to mid 1980 prices — a halfway point in the two-year study. The variation in these four key estimates is striking. The highest estimate was more than four times larger than the lowest. Even if we ignore the replacement cost estimate, a very wide range of potential market value remains.

The Rental Rates. The final stage in the valuation procedure involved the conversion of the stock measure into a rental (flow) measure. For purposes

Table 1. Estimates of the MMHC Facility's Stock Value

Source of Price Estimate (for year)	Price per Square Foot (for site)	Application: Total MMHC 1980 Market Price
Hospital vice-president Purchase price paid (1983) for "comparable" adjacent property	$ 78.83	$8,927,970
State of Massachusetts appraiser: written estimate (1980)	85.73	9,709,051
Expert witness: estimate purchase price for the MMHC (1984) as commercial real estate[a]	24.92	2,821,879
Architect/developer firm: written bid for replacement of MMHC buildings (1980)	117.64	13,323,200

[a] In constructing this price, the witness noted that the owners of adjacent properties might be willing to pay substantially higher rates to obtain the parcel.

Note: All dollar values converted to 1980 dollars using the Consumer Price Index. The MMHC contains 113,254 square feet of space.

of analysis, an average of the two similar estimates—that is, for the appraiser's historical cost estimate—was used as a midpoint value. The estimated replacement cost was the upper bound, while the commercial realtor's price estimate was the lower bound. By taking these three points in a range of market prices, we were able to complete the final stage of modeling the rental rate.

The computation was based on a rewriting of equation 1:

$$N = V \times r$$

where N is net rent, V is the stock value, and r is equal to the rate of return on capital. As defined in the preceding section, N is net of operating costs, including any depreciation on the value of the facility. Using sensitivity analysis, we used the range of values obtained in the study to calculate rental rate parameters. The results are presented in Table 2. The range, while arbitrary, was designed to exhibit the effect of changes in the rate on the value of capital. The low end of the range reflects the argument that the short-run opportunity cost of capital is negligible for an institution that produces a public good. Rental rates along the range imply more conventional rates of return.

To obtain an accurate estimate of rental rate, it was necessary to determine the required rate of return; that is, what the market requires for the use of capital. Depreciation is always a volatile factor, perhaps especially so in the case of aging public facilities. For example, take the case where an asset actually appreciates over time; although its historical cost is paid off (fully depreciated) on the books, it still has alternative uses and these uses have an opportunity cost (Sugden and Williams, 1978).

Impact continues to vary widely under the three scenarios. Clearly, determination of net rental cost is highly sensitive to the rate used. At a minimum, this example illustrates the broad range of possible cost values inherent in analyses of this kind. And, as noted earlier, while the methodology used is sound, it is not elegant; the goal, valuation of capital, was hampered by the absence of market trading and observed market rents. Working backwards, in a sense, from estimates of a stock value for the facility demanded reliance on assumptions at several points. These assumptions weaken the possibility of narrowing the range of values in the outcome table. To put it another way, if this effort had been designed to weight an investment opportunity, it would be difficult to justify a go–no go decision based on a single point in this data range.

Without question, it was necessary to qualify incorporation of the range of capital value estimates into the larger cost-effectiveness evaluation. The viability of the rental rate measure used here depends largely on the accuracy of the information that was gathered. Errors inherent in this indirect approach to capital valuation would be avoided in instances where rent can be observed directly.

Table 2. Rental Rates Under Various Scenarios

Facility	Estimate	Price per square foot	Total (V)	3%	5%	V × r# 7%	9%
MMHC (Commercial Developer)	Lower Bound	$24.92	$2,921,879	$84,656	$141,094	$197,532	$253,969
MMHC (Sale of comparable property)	Midpoint	$83.12	$9,418,290	$282,399	$470,665	$658,930	$847,196
MMHC (Replacement Cost)	Upper Bound	$117.64	$13,323,200	$399,696	$666,160	$932,624	$1,199,088

Concluding Observation

The valuation of capital has been a neglected feature of mental health cost research, and the case study described here highlights the difficulties that can be encountered when the facility is publicly owned. At a minimum, our inability to define a narrow range of estimates of stock value and therefore of rental rates for the Boston facility calls into question the use of analytical models that produce a single estimate of the cost of capital. Although observation of rental rates for public facilities is theoretically correct, it is in fact not usually feasible. Therefore, consideration should be given to other, indirect methods for deriving estimates of the opportunity cost of capital.

Public-sector information needs continue to grow, requiring increasingly refined cost-effectiveness analysis. If the goal of mental health research is a full accounting of the economic costs associated with treatment alternatives, the use of a facility's per diem rate is insufficient. Since information from cost-effectiveness studies will be used to make allocation decisions, the inclusion of a measure of capital cost will increase our understanding of trade-offs. In fact, this chapter has shown that the impact of capital cost on a program comparison can be strong enough to shift the favorable cost outcome from one treatment model to another. Despite the limitations of the methods now available, incorporation of this feature of cost finding ensures that the cost model is comprehensive.

References

Cassell, W., Smith, C., Grunberg, F., Boan, J., and Thomas, P. "Comparing Costs of Hospital and Community Care." *Hospital and Community Psychiatry,* 1972, *23,* 17-20.

Finkler, S. "The Distinction Between Cost and Charges." *Annals of Internal Medicine,* 1982, *96,* 102-109.

McGuire, T., and Dickey, B. "Economic Assessment of Treatment Programs for the Chronically Mentally Ill." Paper presented at a symposium on evaluation of mental health services programs, Stockholm, Sweden, March 23-25, 1983.

May, P. "Cost Efficiency of Treatments for the Schizophrenic Patient." *American Journal of Psychiatry,* 1971, *127,* 1382-1385.

Mosher, L. R. "Alternatives to Psychiatric Hospitalization: Why Has Research Failed to Be Translated into Practice?" *New England Journal of Medicine,* 1983, *309,* 1579-1580.

Rubin, J. "Cost Measurement and Cost Data in Mental Health Settings." *Hospital and Community Psychiatry,* 1980, *33,* 750-754.

Sorensen, J., and Kucic, A. R. *Assessing the Cost Outcomes and Cost Effectiveness of Community Support Programs: Final Report.* Denver: Colorado Division of Mental Health, 1981.

Sugden, R., and Williams, A. *The Principles of Practical Cost-Benefit Analysis.* London: Oxford University Press, 1978.

Vraciw, R. A. "Capital Costs." In G. E. Brisbee and R. A. Vraciw (Eds.), *Managing the Finances of Health Care Organizations.* Ann Arbor, Mich.: Health Administration Press, 1980.

Weisbrod, B. "A Guide to Benefit-Cost Analysis as Seen Through a Controlled Experiment in Treating the Mentally Ill." *Journal of Health Politics, Policy, and Law,* 1983, *7* (4), 808-845.

Weisbrod, B., Test, M. A., and Stein, L. "Alternatives to Mental Hospital Treatment." *Archives of General Psychiatry,* 1980, *37,* 400-405.

Zelman, W., Stone, A., and Davenport, B. "Factors Contributing to Artifactual Differences in Reported Mental Health Costs." *Administration in Mental Health,* 1982, *10,* 40-52.

Nancy L. Cannon is research associate, Massachusetts Mental Health Center, Boston.

Thomas McGuire is associate professor, Department of Economics, Boston University.

Barbara Dickey is assistant professor, Department of Psychiatry, Harvard Medical School.

Cost-benefit analysis and cost-effectiveness analysis are powerful decision-making tools, but they are seldom practiced by evaluators. This recent survey suggests some of the reasons why.

State-Level Evaluation Uses of Cost Analysis: A National Descriptive Survey

Nick L. Smith
Jana K. Smith

A number of authors have argued that evaluators should make more use of cost analysis methods than they do. Indeed, Wortman (1983, p. 256) has gone so far as to state that "knowledge and use of (cost-effectiveness analysis and cost-benefit analysis) may be essential for the very survival of evaluation research." Despite urgent appeals like this, cost analysis methods have been slow to spread, especially in educational evaluation. Since we knew of no formal study of the practice of cost analysis in educational evaluation, we conducted a national survey to identify the types of cost work being done and to study impediments to the use of cost procedures in educational evaluation.

The purpose of this chapter is to provide evidence on the amount and types of cost analysis activities currently done for evaluation purposes in state education agencies (SEAs). We seek to provide a state-of-the-practice report on the use of cost methods by SEAs in evaluating programs and interventions.

The work reported in this chapter was supported in part by a contract to the Northwest Regional Educational Laboratory from the National Institute of Education, but this chapter does not necessarily reflect the position or policy of either agency.

By way of introduction, we review some arguments for the use of cost methods in educational evaluation. We outline four basic types of cost methods. Then we summarize preliminary evidence for their use from a review of the educational literature and from a case study of one firm's cost analysis service contracts.

The main body of this chapter reports the results of a national survey of all evaluation units in state departments of education. For a complete description of the survey, the reader can consult Smith and Smith (1984). The study provided comprehensive information on current practice and future demands for cost work at the state level. The results reveal that, although some cost work is being done, it is simpler and more descriptive than the sophisticated, comparative approaches advocated in the evaluation literature.

The Need for Cost Methods

Although financial resources for education expanded rapidly during the 1960s and early 1970s, a number of factors have combined to change the outlook for the 1980s. Declining tax bases, tax expenditure limitations, school bond and levy failures, continued inflationary pressures, and reductions in the level of state and federal aid have combined to place tremendous stress on educational systems. Evidence indicates that the trend will continue. Resource projections (for example, Kirst and Garms, 1980) suggest that educational revenues will not keep pace with inflation in the 1980s.

Educational personnel struggle to cope with these budgetary problems. Budget reductions have to be made under a variety of constraints, including employee contracts, the interests of political groups, and the quality of the education provided. Further, restrictions on or prohibitions against deficit spending by school districts place additional pressure on school personnel to find places where budget reductions can be made with minimum detrimental impact. Even when budget reductions are not an issue, the public has increasingly demanded analyses of educational costs because tight economic times have heightened public concern for financial accountability.

One possible way of responding to these budgetary problems is to provide information on the relationships between program costs and program outcomes. Historically, educational evaluators have studied program operations (process) or impact (outcomes), but they have not related that information to program costs. They have been able to say which program alternative was more effective, but they do not know whether the increased effectiveness bears any relation to increased cost. Historically, budget managers have based their recommendations on comparative costs, but they have not been able to say whether less costly alternatives were more or less effective. Only by incorporating both costs and outcomes into comparative studies of program alternatives can one reliably determine which alternative is most effective for a given cost or how much it would cost to obtain a desired level of effect (Levin, 1975.)

The general decline in educational resources is having an impact on the practice of educational evaluation, and it appears to be increasing evaluators' concerns with cost analysis methods. Recent studies (Gray and others, 1982; Gray and Smith, 1983) suggest that declining budgets are having a greater impact on evaluation activities than new federal legislation, such as the Education Consolidation and Improvement Act of 1981, and that they are increasing the number of cost analysis questions asked by educational clients.

The relationships between program costs and program effects has thus become increasingly important. Research on educational innovation has repeatedly shown that one prerequisite to successful adaption of new approaches is the presence of locally felt need (Berman and McLaughlin, 1975; Cheever and others, 1976; Fullen and Pomfret, 1975). At present there appears to be some evidence of locally felt need for increased use of cost analysis techniques in educational evaluation.

Types of Cost Methods

A variety of methods can be used for dealing with cost problems in educational evaluation, such as operations research (Page, 1979; Wholeben and Sullivan, 1982) or management consultation procedures (for example, Stanfield, 1982), but applied economists have argued that the methods of greatest analytic usefulness are likely to be cost-benefit, cost-effectiveness, and cost-utility analyses. These approaches enable one to combine outcomes with costs to determine the most effective and efficient program options. Cost-feasibility analysis can also be a useful planning method, although it does not combine outcomes with costs.

Levin (1975, 1981, 1983) provides an excellent introduction to the use of these four methods in evaluation. Although we subsequently found it necessary to consider additional, simpler types of cost-analysis procedures, Levin's descriptions helped us to frame our first questions about the use of cost procedures in evaluation.

Cost-feasibility analysis involves estimating whether the cost of a program alternative is within existing financial resources. Cost-feasibility analysis does not incorporate program outcomes and therefore provides no way of combining costs and outcomes in an overall analysis as the other three methods do. Because cost-utility analysis involves the subjective measurement of probable outcomes, its results are often not replicable, and it therefore provides only a weak basis for programmatic decisions. By expressing all outcomes in terms of dollars, cost-benefit analysis provides replicable results and enables us not only to compare alternatives for a given program but to compare across programs that have different classes of outcomes. However, it often is difficult to assign monetary values to such educational program outcomes as enhanced music appreciation, reading comprehension, or self-confidence. As a result, cost-benefit studies have been difficult to do, and they have traditionally had little credibility at the local level.

Cost-effectiveness analysis represents program outcomes in terms not of monetary units but of other effectiveness units, such as reading scores, attitude scale scores, behavioral rates, or other standard outcome measures currently used in educational evaluation. Because we do not convert all outcomes into the same unit (dollars), we cannot use cost-effectiveness analysis to compare programs of different types (for example, to compare reading programs with athletic programs), but it does enable us to compare programs with similar outcomes, such as two reading improvement progams.

Of the available techniques, therefore, cost-effectiveness analysis seems to be the most suitable for cost evaluations of educational programs. To what extent is it currently being used? We turned to the educational literature for information on that question.

Review of Literature

In order to identify current practices in the use of cost-effectiveness analysis in educational evaluation, we searched for published studies that used it. We started by searching all ERIC entries from 1977 to 1983; then we searched the references cited in the articles obtained from the ERIC search.

We found several articles and books urging evaluators to use cost-effectiveness analysis. Some reviewed previous uses of cost methods. Alkin (1970) advocates the use of cost analysis in the evaluation of instructional programs. Levin (1975) provides an introduction to cost analysis as well as a brief overview of cost-effectiveness and cost-benefit methods in studies of such educational topics as manpower training programs, teacher selection, computer-assisted instruction, dropouts, preschool programs, and compensatory education. Levin (1981) examines seven illustrative studies of the use of cost-benefit and cost-effectiveness analysis in education critically; he uses examples from many of the same areas. Levin (1983) and Thompson (1980) have written texts on the use of cost-effectiveness and cost-benefit analyses in evaluation. One recent addition to the literature is a volume on cost-effectiveness studies of educational evaluations themselves (Alkin and Solmon, 1983). Other authors (Lorenzen and Braskamp, 1978; Carr and others, 1982; Klees and Wells, 1983) have dealt with the problems and benefits of using cost-effectiveness and cost-benefit analyses in evaluation.

Unfortunately, we found few evaluations that used cost-effectiveness analysis to make comparative judgments about program or intervention alternatives. A good example of the type of cost-effectiveness application for which we were searching is the study by Quinn and others (1984) of the cost effectiveness of two different programs for teaching fifth-grade math. Quinn and colleagues used identical costs and effects measures to analyze the effectiveness of two in-place math programs. In general, however, we found very few such studies. Some articles had misleading titles; they did not actually deal with cost-effectiveness analysis. Others discussed cost-effectiveness issues without presenting results, or they presented results based on subjective judgments, not on empirical evidence.

Other reviewers of this literature have found similar results. For example, in a review of compensatory education evaluations, Mullin and Summers (1983) found that only eight of the forty-seven studies they examined had looked at the relationships between costs and program effects. Wargo and others (1972) found thirty-eight studies of compensatory education that claimed to look at cost-effectiveness issues, but thirty-two had done so on a purely subjective basis.

Although we found very few cost-effectiveness studies of program alternatives in the educational literature, we did find studies that looked at costs only and paid no attention to effects (Smith and Hendrickson, 1982; Andersen, 1982; Hartman, 1981). Of course, most evaluations, whether they include studies of cost or not, are not published in the educational literature; instead, they are used as in-house documents for managerial purposes. While we had expected the literature review to underestimate the incidence of cost studies in educational evaluation, we were surprised at how few studies we did find. Further, in discussing our literature review with evaluation practitioners who have conducted cost studies, we came to suspect that the traditional cost-analysis methods are inappropriate for managerial purposes in educational program evaluation settings. Therefore, to appreciate the nature and purpose of the cost studies that were actually being performed in educational evaluation, we conducted a case study of the cost-analysis work being done by an educational firm that did evaluation contracting.

An Evaluation Contracting Firm: A Case Study

We identified and analyzed all cost studies (fifteen) done over a five-year period, from 1977 through 1982, by a regional, private research and development agency as a part of its evaluation service work. These studies were conducted for school districts and state departments of education. Smith (1983) describes this study in detail.

The studies were identified by talking with agency staff about their own past and current cost projects and by asking about other staff in the agency who might have been involved in such work. The published report of each cost study was abstracted according to a standard case study report form, and the study's principal investigator was interviewed to confirm the accuracy of the abstracted description and to clarify points in the written report that were not clear. The final list of abstracted cost studies was reviewed by agency administrators to ensure that all major cost studies had been identified and properly described.

For each study, the following information was collected: report title, client, year of the study, budget allocated to the study, length of time taken to complete the study, and length of the report. The studies ranged in cost from

$1,666 to $75,000 and took between two weeks and thirty-six months to complete. The reports ran from five to three hundred and fifty pages. Four of the studies were done for local education agencies, three for state education agencies, and two were reported jointly to clients of both types. Six studies were conducted specifically for chief state school officers.

Each cost analysis study was reviewed to identify the decision context, to describe the cost methods used, and to critique the application of cost procedures. The completed case studies were sorted into categories according to type of cost problem. Four categories were identified: cost comparisons between two or more programs or entities (five studies), cost descriptions of a single program or entity (three studies), budgets and planning (three studies), and policy analyses (four studies).

This review of fifteen cost analysis investigations uncovered no cost-effectiveness studies. Rather, only simple cost descriptions or cost comparisons were found. Why were simple cost questions consistently posed in lieu of questions involving effectiveness or benefits, especially when, as in many cases, a more powerful cost method could have been used to analyze existing data? To answer this question, we explored the formulation of the original cost question posed by the educator or client in these studies, since the client's question had played a large part in determining the particular cost analysis method used.

In general, we found that relatively complicated cost analyses were not conducted for four reasons: The client did not know how to ask such cost questions, the client felt no need for information about the relationship between program effects and program costs, the client did not feel that it was possible to conduct cost-effectiveness or cost-benefit studies, or the client did not view his or her setting in terms of comparative cost-effects relationships.

Subsequently, twenty-two evaluators and educators from contracting firms, universities, local school districts, and state departments of education gathered to critique and interpret the case study's findings. The consensus of conference participants was that, first, although many evaluators and educational administrators know little about formal cost analysis procedures, evaluative cost studies are needed; second, a few local and state agencies are already conducting such studies, probably more than the journal literature suggests, but the study reports are fugitive documents; third, the four formal cost analysis methods pose serious feasibility problems, and adapted or simplified procedures may be needed; fourth, cost problems usually involve more than the analysis of costs and outcomes; such issues as state appropriations and local bond elections are more salient for educational administrators than cost-effect ratios.

As a result of these preliminary investigations, we were able to conduct a systematic survey of the use of the various forms of cost analysis now being used in educational evaluation and to identify the major impediments to implementation of such methods in state education agencies. This work is described in the next section.

The National Survey

Background. In 1983, a mailed questionnaire survey was conducted of all fifty state departments of education. The purpose of the study was to record the types of cost studies that state-level evaluation units were conducting, the need for future applications of cost methods, and existing impediments to the use of cost analysis methods. Although almost all state education agencies have some personnel with evaluation responsibilities, we were interested in the formal cost studies conducted by states with centralized program evaluation units.

Thirty-seven states had centralized evaluation units in 1983, and twenty-nine (78 percent) provided data for our study. State population data, school enrollment figures, and direct telephone interviews with SEA personnel were used to make bias checks of nonrespondents. Nonresponding states tended to have smaller state populations and school enrollments than responding states, and they were more similar to states without evaluation units than to the responding states. The data reported here are, therefore, slightly biased in favor of the more populous states that have centralized evaluation units.

Descriptive information on these evaluation units revealed a range of from one to ninety in-house evaluations conducted per year by one to thirty-seven full-time professional staff. The average unit conducted about eight evaluations a year and had a professional staff of seven. These data were compared with similar information collected five years earlier. There appear to have been substantial reductions over the five-year period in the size of SEA evaluation units. While the majority of studies continues to be conducted in-house, far fewer evaluations are being performed. Although the differences among individual state units in number of staff and evaluations conducted seem to be decreasing, the individual units still respond to a diverse set of multiple responsibilities, which range from consultation to evaluation monitoring and policy analysis. Smith (1984) provides more information.

The results of the mail survey are presented in the next section. We start by discussing the current level of practice. We move on to the anticipated need for future studies, and we close with a review of impediments to the use of cost methods.

Study Results. First, we asked the evaluation units how many cost studies they had performed in the past five years for each of seven different purposes. The list of purposes was based on our past studies of practice and the literature. It is displayed in Table 1. Purposes are ranked in increasing order of complexity along with their reported levels of use. Single cost descriptions and cost-feasibility analyses were the types of studies most commonly done. Although a few evaluation units had done as many as a dozen studies in the past five years, the mode for each category was clearly zero.

Respondents were asked to describe the most important cost studies they had conducted in the last five years. They reported on twenty-four differ-

Table 1. Cost Studies Conducted by State-Level Evaluation Units in the Past Five Years

Purpose of Study	Number of Studies Mean	Range
Single Cost Description To describe the costs of a single existing program	1.80	0–5
Cost-Feasibility Analysis To see whether a planned program is affordable within the resources available	1.47	0–15
Cost-Utility Analysis To compare the costs of a planned program with its estimated outcomes	0.59	0–10
Single Cost-Outcome Description To compare the costs with outcomes of a single existing program	0.93	0–6
Multiple Cost Descriptions To compare the costs of two or more existing programs	0.14	0–1
Cost-Effectiveness Analysis To compare the costs with outcomes of two or more existing programs where outcomes are measured in test scores, ratings, and so forth	0.35	0–5
Cost-Benefit Analysis To compare the costs with outcomes of two or more existing programs where both outcomes and costs are measured in dollars	0.31	0–5

ent studies. The topics of these studies were evenly divided between educational programs (math, reading, vocational education, compensatory education, community education, and so forth) and support services (data processing, media, personnel, assessment, and so forth). Again, the method most often used was the single cost description; it was followed by cost-feasibility analysis. In twenty cases, the studies were reported as having resulted in important feedback or program changes. Fifteen respondents commented on the value of their cost studies; thirteen thought that the studies had been valuable and effective. Thus, although the incidence of cost studies has been low and the methods used have been relatively simple, the evaluation units that have done the studies have generally been pleased with their efforts.

When respondents were asked whether there was currently a formal expectation or requirement within the state agency that the evaluation unit do some form of cost analysis work, a surprising 48.3 percent said yes. While eleven of the units currently devoted no resources to cost studies, the other seventeen units that responded devoted an average of 11.5 percent of their budget to cost work. When respondents were asked whether they anticipated that there would be a formal expectation or requirement for cost analysis work over the next five years, 58.6 percent said yes and anticipated that they would have to spend an average 17 percent of their budgets on cost studies. Therefore, more state-level evaluation units expect to be required to do cost studies in the future than do not, and more anticipate having to spend a greater share of their resources on cost-analysis work.

Next, we asked the evaluation units how many of the seven types of cost studies listed in Table 1 they anticipated doing over the next five years. Figure 1 compares current with anticipated use of the seven types of cost studies. Evaluation personnel expect to do more of all but the simplest procedure, single cost description; the greatest increases involve cost-utility analysis (18.3 percent increase) and cost-feasibility analysis (14.8 percent increase). Neither of these two approaches includes direct assessment of outcomes. The cost-effectiveness method does; the expected increase for that method was more modest (about 11 percent). Thus, while demand for cost analysis may increase, and more evaluation resources may be devoted to such studies, the complexity of the methods used may not increase appreciably.

Even though almost 60 percent of the state-level evaluation units anticipated doing cost studies in the future, they expected to be using the ostensible cost method of choice, cost-effectiveness analysis, only about a quarter of the time. What are the impediments to cost studies in state-level settings? What are the impediments to the use of cost-effectiveness analysis? We addressed those issues.

By studying the literature, examining examples of cost analysis service work, and discussing the problems posed by cost analysis methods with evaluators, clients, and economists, we developed a list of impediments to the use of cost methods. Our original list contained fifty-one items; twenty-one items were grouped together as resource and organizational constraints, and thirty items were grouped as methodological and technical inadequacies. We reduced our list to twenty items, ten in each category; then we used the results of field tests to reduce the list once again to a total of fourteen items. We asked survey participants to respond to this list of impediments. The results are summarized in Table 2.

The three highest-ranked impediments to cost analysis were item *a* ("We are seldom asked to do cost studies"), item *i* ("It is difficult to relate cost data to educational outcomes"), and item *n* ("We have few guidebooks, texts, or examples to follow in conducting cost studies"). Respondents were least able to decide (that is, they marked "Don't Know") whether it was possible to include all important cost factors in an analysis (item *g*) and whether consultants or experts were available to help with cost problems (item *l*). A reliability coefficient (standardized item α) was computed for this scale; only the observations on which complete data were available ($N = 20$) were used. The reliability coefficient was .64. The most highly intercorrelated items were items *d* and *e* (.72) — studies cost too much, and studies take too much time — items *b* and *c* (.70) — decision makers are not interested in cost results, and decision makers do not use cost results — and items *a* and *b* (.66) — decision makers are not interested in cost results, and decision makers do not ask for cost studies.

Because cost-effectiveness analysis of often advocated as the best method for educational evaluation, we asked a similar question specifically

Figure 1. Percent of State-Level Evaluation Units Using Cost Analysis Methods

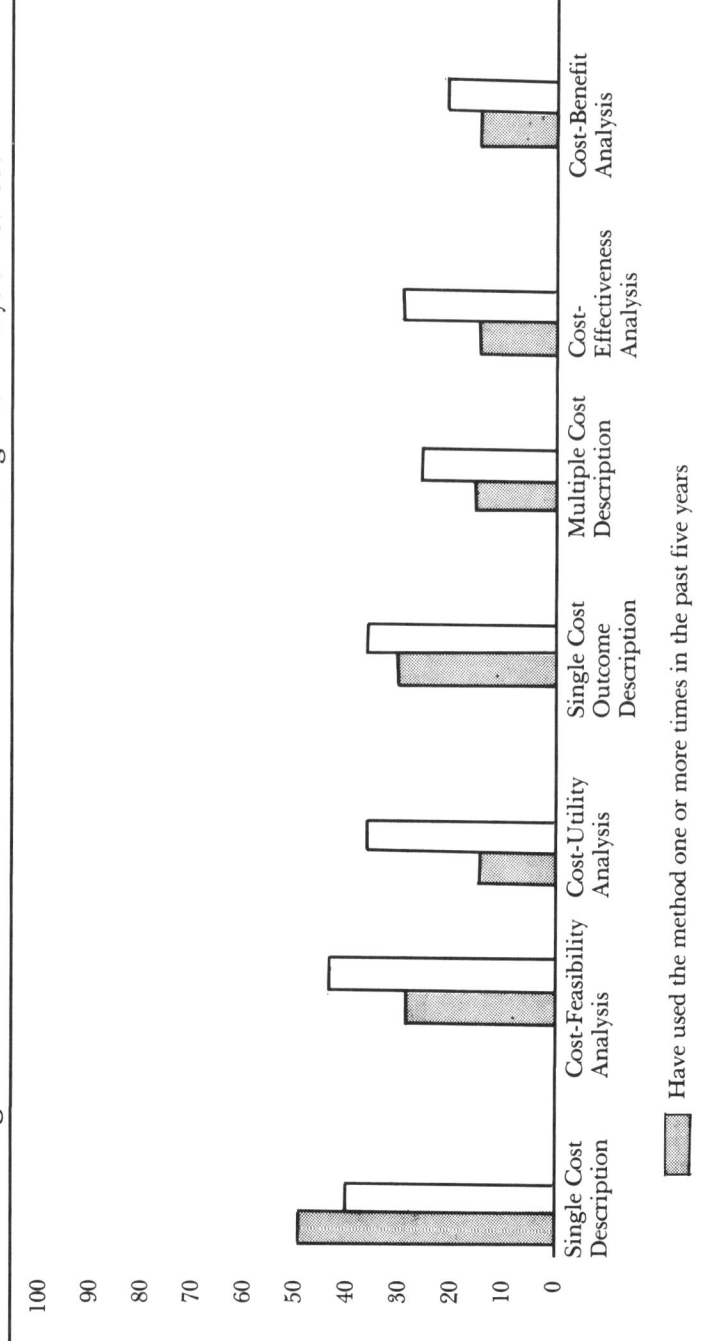

Table 2. Impediments to the Use of Cost Analysis in State-Level Evaluation Units

Item		Mean[a]	Don't Know
a.	We are seldom asked to do cost studies	3.00	1
b.	Decision makers are not often interested in actual cost information.	2.28	0
c.	Decision makers do not often use the results of cost studies.	2.30	2
d.	It takes too much time to conduct cost studies.	2.37	2
e.	It costs too much to conduct cost studies.	2.22	2
f.	Accurate cost data are usually not available.	2.71	1
g.	Cost study results are incomplete because it is not possible to include all important cost factors.	2.69	3
h.	Accurate outcome data are usually not available.	2.69	0
i.	It is difficult to relate cost data to educational outcomes.	3.00	0
j.	Cost results do not tell managers how to improve program operations.	2.43	1
k.	We lack staff with the technical capability to conduct cost studies.	2.45	0
l.	We lack available consultants or experts to help us conduct cost studies.	2.31	3
m.	We do not have sufficient experience in conducting cost studies.	2.66	0
n.	We have few guidebooks, texts, or examples to follow in conducting cost studies.	2.82	1

[a] 4=Strongly Agree, 3=Agree, 2=Disagree, 1=Strongly Disagree. The mean is based on an N of 29 minus the number of Don't Knows.

about impediments to its use. Responses to that question are summarized in Table 3. Respondents were less critical of any individual impediment than they had been in the previous question. The greatest impediments to the use of cost-effectiveness analysis were item *g* ("Cost-effectiveness analysis is difficult to do because of technical details [for example, discount rates] and the need for sophisticated analysis procedures"), item *e* ("Cost-effectiveness analysis considers only a limited number of program outcomes and so does not represent true program effects"), and item *b* ("Cost-effectiveness analysis is often not feasible because comparative program studies are seldom possible").

Using only responses with complete data ($N = 17$), we calculated a standardized item α coefficient for this scale: .73. The highest intercorrelations were between items *g* and *h* (.74) — cost-effectiveness analysis needs more development, and cost-effectiveness analysis is too technical — items *e* and *h* (.74) — cost-effectiveness analysis needs more development, and cost-effectiveness analysis considers only a limited number of outcomes — and items *b* and *c* (.71) — cost-effectiveness analysis is too specialized, and cost-effectiveness analysis is often not feasible.

Table 3. Impediments to the Use of Cost-Effectiveness Analysis in State-Level Evaluation Units

Item		Mean[a]	Don't Know
a.	Cost-effectiveness analysis is often unnecessary because decision makers are not interested in relating program costs and effects.	2.38	0
b.	Cost-effectiveness analysis is often not feasible because comparative program studies are seldom possible.	2.44	2
c.	Cost-effectiveness analysis is too specialized a technique to be generally applicable.	2.08	4
d.	Cost-effectiveness analysis is so costly and complex that it is warranted only for major studies.	2.35	6
e.	Cost-effectiveness analysis considers only a limited number of program outcomes and so does not represent true program effects.	2.45	9
f.	Cost-effectiveness analysis is of limited utility since it provides no information on program procedures or local conditions.	2.24	4
g.	Cost-effectiveness analysis is difficult to do because of technical details (for example, discount rates) and the need for sophisticated analysis procedures.	2.56	4
h.	Cost-effectiveness analysis cannot be applied to educational programs without further development of the method.	2.25	5

[a] 4=Strongly Agree, 3=Agree, 2=Disagree, 1=Strongly Disagree. The mean is based on an N of 29 minus the number of Don't Knows.

The responses summarized in Table 2 suggest that the use of cost methods will increase in state-level evaluation work, especially for the simpler methods. The major impediments include not being asked to do such studies (which appears to be changing), the technical difficulty of relating costs to outcomes, and the lack of supporting guidebooks and examples. The situation is somewhat different for cost-effectiveness analysis. There is greater uniformity of response (as Table 3 shows, the range of means for cost-effectiveness analysis spans only .48 points, as compared with .78 points for cost analysis in general), and no particular impediment seems to be a major problem. Although fewer evaluation units expect to be increasing their use of cost-effectiveness analysis, they do not cite major impediments to its use. Why might this be so?

Notice that the number of "Don't Know" responses increases for cost-effectiveness analysis. These educational evaluators appear to have felt that they knew less about cost-effectiveness analysis than they did about cost analysis in general. In a separate question, we asked respondents to indicate their highest level of familiarity with cost-effectiveness analysis. We gave them four choices: I have no knowledge of it, I have minimal familiarity with it, I have read about it or studied it, and I have conducted studies using it. Eighteen (62 percent) of the respondents reported having studied or used the techniques, while the remaining eleven (38 percent) said they knew little or nothing about it. Perhaps the data in Table 3 reflect two different groups of evaluators: Some units know little about the technique and so marked "Don't Know," while others were familiar with the technique and reported that none of the possible impediments was a major obstacle; that is, the means in Table 3 (2.34 average) are lower than they are in Table 2 (2.57 average).

Several other correlations support this possible two-group explanation. There is a significant relationship between the total number of cost studies that a unit has done in the past five years and the number that it expects to do over the next five years ($r = .69$, significant at $p = .001$), and there is an extremely strong relationship between units that have had formal expectations of cost work and units that anticipate future demands ($r = .94$, significant at $p = .001$). Further, those units that most expect to use cost-effectiveness analysis in the future are those that have done the most cost work in the past ($r = .63$, significant at $p = .001$) or that have used cost-effectiveness procedures most in the past ($r = .49$, significant at $p = .003$). Finally, we recoded the data summarized in Tables 2 and 3 to compute a general cost analysis impediments index and a specific cost-effectiveness impediments index. These two indexes, in general, reflect the perceived magnitude of the problems that state-level evaluation units feel they must overcome in order to conduct cost studies. There is a moderate, positive correlation between these two indexes ($r = .31$, significant at $p = .049$), suggesting that units that feel major impediments to the use of cost analysis in general also feel impediments to the use of the cost-effectiveness technique.

Summary. In general, we can summarize the major findings of our survey as well as of the background work that preceded it as follows: The educational literature contains few cost analysis studies of educational programs. Most studies appear to have been conducted for internal management purposes. Our case study of the contracting firm's use of cost analysis suggests that only the simpler cost methods are being used, perhaps in part because clients do not know enough to ask for more complex analyses, because they do not want to relate costs to outcomes, because they do not consider complex cost studies feasible, or because they think less in terms of comparative trials than in terms of midcourse corrections of single programs. Further, the case study suggests that there may be more fugitive, management uses of cost analysis than are generally known, despite major feasibility problems with the more complex methods.

Our study of state-level evaluation units confirms that some units are doing cost work and that many are under formal obligations to do so. They expect these obligations to increase and anticipate that they will be doing more cost studies in the near future. These units expect to be using slightly more complex methods, but they do not anticipate extensive use of the theoretical method of choice, cost-effectiveness analysis.

The biggest impediments to the doing of more cost work in state-level evaluation units, aside from the absence of requests for such work, is the difficulty of relating costs to outcomes and the absence of texts and examples to guide the work. The major impediment to the use of cost-effectiveness analysis is its complexity, although many of the respondents seem not to have enough knowledge of this technique to comment on impediments to its use.

References

Alkin, M. C. "Evaluating the Cost Effectiveness of Instructional Programs." In M. C. Wittrock and D. E. Wiley (Eds.), *The Evaluation of Instruction: Issues and Problems.* New York: Holt, Rinehart & Winston, 1970.

Alkin, M. C., and Solmon, L. C. (Eds.). *The Costs of Evaluation.* Beverly Hills, Calif.: Sage, 1983.

Andersen, D. F. "Problems in Estimating the Costs of Special Education in Urban Areas: The New York City Case." *Journal of Education Finance,* 1982, *7,* 403-424.

Berman, P., and McLaughlin, M. W. *Federal Programs Supporting Educational Change.* Vol. 6: *The Findings in Review.* Santa Monica, Calif.: Rand Corporation, 1975.

Carr, C., Castilhos, M., Davis, D., Snyder, M., and Stecker, B. "Cost-Benefit Analysis in Educational Evaluation." *Studies in Educational Evaluation,* 1982, *8* (1), 75-85.

Cheever, J., Neill, S. B., and Quinn, J. *Transferring Success.* San Francisco: Far West Laboratory for Educational Research and Development, 1976.

Fullen, M., and Pomfret, A. *Review of Research on Curriculum Implementation.* Ontario: Ontario Institute for Studies in Education, 1975.

Gray, P. J., and Smith, J. K. *Needs Assessment Survey: Cost Analysis, Policy Analysis, and Other Evaluation Methods.* Research on Evaluation Program Paper and Report Series No. 81. Portland, Ore.: Northwest Regional Educational Laboratory, 1983.

Gray, P. J., Caulley, D. N., and Smith, N. L. *A Study in Contrasts: Effects of the Education Consolidation and Improvement Act of 1981 on SEA and LEA Evaluation.* Research on Evaluation Program Paper and Report Series No. 79. Portland, Ore.: Northwest Regional Educational Laboratory, 1982.

Hartman, W. T. "Estimating the Costs of Educating Handicapped Children: A Resource-Cost Model Approach. Summary Report." *Educational Evaluation and Policy Analysis,* 1981, *3* (4), 33-47.

Kirst, M., and Garms, W. "Public School Finance in the 1980s." *Education Digest,* 1980, *46,* 5-8.

Klees, S. J., and Wells, S. J. "Economic Evaluation of Education: A Critical Analysis in the Context of Applications to Educational Reform in El Salvador." *Educational Evaluation and Policy Analysis,* 1983, *5* (3), 327-345.

Levin, H. M. "Cost-Effectiveness Analysis in Evaluation Research." In M. Guttentag and E. Struening (Eds.), *Handbook of Evaluation Research.* Vol. 2. Beverly Hills, Calif.: Sage, 1975.

Levin, H. M. "Cost Analysis." In N. L. Smith (Ed.), *New Techniques for Evaluation.* Beverly Hills, Calif.: Sage, 1981.

Levin, H. M. *Cost Effectiveness: A Primer.* Beverly Hills, Calif.: Sage, 1983.

Lorenzen, G. L., and Braskamp, L. A. "Comparative Influence of Political, Cost-Benefit, and Statistical Information on Administrative Decision Making." *Evaluation and Program Planning,* 1978, *1,* 235-238.

Mullin, S. P., and Summers, A. A. "Is More Better? The Effectiveness of Spending on Compensatory Education." *Phi Delta Kappan,* 1983, *64* (5), 339-347.

Page, E. B. *Educational Evaluation Through Operations Research.* Research on Evaluation Program Paper and Report Series No. 30. Portland, Ore.: Northwest Regional Educational Laboratory, 1979.

Quinn, B., Van Mondfrans, A., and Worthen, B. R. "Cost Effectiveness of Two Math Programs as Moderated by Pupil SES." *Educational Evaluation and Policy Analysis,* 1984, *6* (1), 39-52.

Smith, J. K. *Case Reports of Northwest Regional Educational Laboratory Cost Studies.* Research on Evaluation Program Paper and Report Series No. 82. Portland, Ore.: Northwest Regional Educational Laboratory, 1983.

Smith, M. C., and Hendrickson, L. S. "Evaluating the Cost of School Health Services: A Case Study." *Educational Evaluation and Policy Analysis,* 1982, *4* (4), 527-534.

Smith, N. L. "Evaluation Units in State Departments of Education: A Five-Year Update." *Evaluation News,* 1984, *5* (3), 37-44.

Smith, N. L., and Smith, J. K. *Cost Analysis in Educational Evaluation.* Research on Evaluation Program Paper and Report Series No. 100. Portland, Ore.: Northwest Regional Educational Laboratory, 1984.

Stanfield, J. *Pilot Field Study of SEA Evaluation Costs.* Research on Evaluation Program Paper and Report Series No. 69. Portland, Ore.: Northwest Regional Educational Laboratory, 1982.

Thompson, M. S. *Benefit-Cost Analysis for Program Evaluation.* Beverly Hills, Calif.: Sage, 1980.

Wargo, M. J., and others. *ESEA Title I: A Reanalysis of Synthesis of Evaluation Data from Fiscal Year 1965 Through 1970.* Palo Alto, Calif.: American Institutes for Research, 1972.

Wholeben, B. E., and Sullivan, J. M. *Multiple Alternatives Modeling in Determining Fiscal Rollbacks During Educational Funding Crises.* Research on Evaluation Program Paper and Report Series No. 70. Portland, Ore.: Northwest Regional Educational Laboratory, 1982.

Wortman, P. M. "Evaluation Research: A Methodological Perspective." *Annual Review of Psychology,* 1983, *34,* 223-260.

Zaltman, G., Florio, D., and Sikorski, L. *Dynamic Educational Change: Models, Strategies, Tactics, and Management.* New York: Free Press, 1977.

Nick L. Smith is director, Research on Evaluation Program, Northwest Regional Educational Laboratory.

Jana K. Smith is evaluation specialist, Research on Evaluation Program, Northwest Regional Educational Laboratory.

What do the preceding chapters suggest about the role of economic analysis in program evaluation, and where might efforts to improve these tools be concentrated?

Economic Directions for Program Evaluation

James S. Catterall

At the outset of this volume, I promised readers meaningful exposure to economics-based models that were relevant to the goals of public program evaluation. Here I will attempt to draw together the central themes that our authors have brought to this task. What economic constructs and ways of interpreting the world have been shown that provide bridges to common traditions in the field of program evaluation? What areas have we neglected? I will point to areas that seem particularly deserving of our next efforts to improve these skills and their applications.

Economics and Program Evaluation

We can begin by reminding ourselves of the fundamental problems that economists address in their work and of the bond between that work and the goals of program evaluation. Economists examine problems related to the allocation of scarce resources in society. What and how much is produced and who benefits from this production are the fundamental questions tied to resource allocation. Concerns about the distribution of income and wealth, the mix of public and private activity in efforts to achieve our ends, and the financing of the activities pursued through public enterprises are closely related to these questions.

The program evaluation is largely assumed to be connected in one way or another with public institutions that produce services and goods—health care, welfare, housing, transportation, and education, to name a few. The evaluator is further presumed to concentrate on identifying and gauging the various effects of public interventions so that the programs that work best can be singled out or so that programs to which we have commitments can be improved. The assumption of a public connection is made primarily because public institutions and the legislative bodies that spawn and maintain them have created a corps of professional evaluators who are either on the staff of the institutions in question or who consult or contract research relationships with them. The assumption is made also because evaluators do in practice largely focus their attention on the various enterprises of our public institutions.

As I discussed in the Editor's Notes, the critical overlap between these two worlds is the desire of all involved to improve or even optimize resource allocation. This means that, when we pursue a task, we hope to find a way that gets us further along toward our goals or that garners more of what we seek, given what we are willing to apply to seeking it. Or, to put it another way, we wish to minimize the resources or costs that we must commit to a goal in order to achieve it. In short, a common goal of the sort of public policy analysis that we describe is maximization of product or service, given a budget, or minimization of costs, given a set of goals.

The work of both evaluators and economists has helped to resolve the problems posed by social resource allocation and optimization. First, we must have ways of gauging the effects of programs, of understanding how they work, and of deciding how they can be improved. The evaluation profession has long toiled in this field. Second, we must also sense the resource commitments that alternative program choices imply. Economists have developed techniques both for assessing costs and for synthesizing measures of costs and effects. The authors of the chapters in this sourcebook underscore the fundamental linkages between economic models and program evaluation and some of the important building blocks needed in order to realize the analytical ideals described here. The next section highlights the contributions of our authors.

The Contributions of Our Authors

Chapter One is a clear, tightly written, and comprehensive economic analysis of one important question facing our society: As our industries regroup in order to modernize or in response to cyclical downturns, what role can public authorities play in helping displaced workers to find productive employment? Kulik, Smith, and Stromsdorfer probe the relative merits of job placement and retraining strategies in the context of large-scale efforts in the Detroit area to reemploy laid-off auto workers. They broach a host of troublesome research design questions expertly and instructively in their discussion. The authors' handling of possible selection bias on the part of participants, their recognition of the importance of possible interactions between program treatments and other resources that participants draw on to help with their predicaments, their sensitivity to subtle issues of experimental control, and their overall attention to potential sources of bias in their estimates are exemplary.

Of still more interest to the core issue of this sourcebook is their work in two other areas: the nature of the economic outcomes evaluated and the potential importance of costs in program choices. Economic outcomes are important to many public programs. Education, training, welfare services, rehabilitative services, and counseling efforts attached to public programs and a variety of additional public services all include successful employment and self-sufficiency for participants among their goals. Program evaluation in these areas must of necessity attend to such economic outcomes, and this first chapter articulates an effective scheme for doing so. Kulik, Smith, and Stromsdorfer carefully specify the nature of the various economic outcomes sought. For their analysis, the measurement of employment in alternative ways was critical in capturing a sense of whether the assistance provided for displaced workers was yielding effects. Attaining a job at all, the amount of time spent working after completing the program, and the subsequent earnings of participants are different and important components of success for such interventions, and each must be approached for a successful evaluation of the questions sought in this study.

Finally, the authors of Chapter One are sensitive to questions of program costs and their links to effects. The fact that job-training strategies were reported to entail costs approximately twice those of placement strategies is of great importance to a discussion of how their relative degrees of effectiveness might bear on public decisions to offer one or the other when faced with problems of worker displacement.

The evaluation design presented by Garfinkel and Corbett in Chapter Two provides another set of ties between program evaluation and economic analysis. The chapter presents an economic analysis that has both formative and summative components, to use the traditional parlance of the program evaluator. Not only is an array of economic and behavioral outcomes slated for assessment (that is, the income maintenance of children and the compliance behavior of those ordered to provide it), but the inquiry has been designed to examine both the success of alternative reform strategies and to provide clues about how the strategies experimented with can be improved. The effects of alternatives on program costs are also critical in the proposed evaluation design.

Chapter Two also illustrates economic analysis of another, but intimately related, sort. The many discussions of possible and alternative inquiry strategies are framed as economic problems. What trade-offs are to be expected in terms of information gains on the one hand and of evaluation costs on the other when such decisions as the number and nature of interviews and surveys are made, or when the number of participating settings is established, or when one design provides information within a year and another only after a much longer time? These are resource allocation problems akin to our central concerns, only here they are writ small, and as a result they are easy to scrutinize. Finally, Garfinkel and Corbett provide a useful and practical discussion of an extended range of data sources relevant to the evaluation at hand.

Nagel's discussion in Chapter Three overlaps the central problems of the economic evaluation of public programs in two ways. First, evaluators usually confront thorny problems when programs involve more than one outcome, as they so often do. When the outcomes of alternative programs do not point toward an unambiguous favorite (that is, when no alternative is shown to be superior to others in all outcome criteria), we have to think further about how we value different mixes of outcomes before we can identify preferences for the interventions involved. Nagel presents several strategies for valuing such mixes and in doing so suggests possible resolutions for this classical problem of program evaluation.

Nagel's formulations also have promise for efforts to link costs to program decision making. Chapter Five reveals that one persistent difficulty cited by those who would apply cost-benefit analysis to many realms of public service is that it is often difficult to equate program outcomes with dollar values. Such equating is required by the cost-benefit analysis model. The notion of monetizing benefits that Nagel discusses in Chapter Three seems to hold promise in this regard. Those who use Nagel's paired comparisons or any of the other devices that he discusses may find their assessments newly amenable to the techniques of cost-benefit analysis.

In Chapter Four, Cannon, McGuire, and Dickey tackle a substantial problem in the assessment of program costs. The evaluator often neglects questions of capital costs for a number of reasons. First, evaluators usually do not treat costs at all or in any depth; as we have stressed, evaluations customarily concentrate on outcomes and program processes. Evaluations that do assess costs often approach them from the perspective of the client's budget. When the provider of a program is using a building that has already been paid for (or that is in the process of being paid for) the cost of capital is often simply ignored. The cost from the point of view of the provider may not be considered to be a relevant variable when decisions about a facility's use are made.

However, from the standpoint of the optimization of social resource allocation, capital costs are important. The use of buildings entails an opportunity cost; an engaged facility cannot be used for other purposes that have demonstrable value. Chapter Four presents the standard ways in which economists estimate capital costs and shows both how substantial capital costs can be in the case of health care and also how sensitive cost estimates are to the methods used to develop them.

Finally, questions of capital costs seem to have great currency nowadays. A cornerstone of Reagan administration policies seems to be the investigation of private alternatives to traditionally public services. In the case of many institutions, such as hospitals and schools, the extensive capital costs involved in the provision of services should be drawn into deliberations over program alternatives.

Finally, Chapter Five surveys a critical and, we hope, emerging area in which economics and program evaluation demonstrate worthwhile ties, the area of program cost analysis. Smith and Smith present a basic rationale for the application of cost-effectiveness analysis to program decision making and single it out for further attention. Chapter Five outlines the four principal models for program costs analysis: cost accounting, cost-benefit analysis, cost-effectiveness analysis, and cost-utility analysis. The chapter references orient readers to a literature that is capable of guiding evaluators further into the practical issues of application.

The survey of uses of cost analysis in educational evaluation presented by Smith and Smith points to the case that I will make in concluding. Cost-effectiveness analysis is a very powerful tool, and it represents a straightforward and achievable extension of program evaluation. Yet, if the world of program evaluation in education offers any valid indication, cost analysis models have yet to make much of a mark on the profession or its practice. Once again, information regarding the outcomes or effects of interventions is necessary for the making of sound policy choices, but it is not in itself sufficient. A step toward sufficiency is taken when information about the outcomes of program alternatives is combined with information about the costs of maintaining those alternatives.

The authors of the chapters in this *New Directions for Program Evaluation* sourcebook hope that their work will inspire some agreement on these points among readers.

James S. Catterall is assistant professor of educational administration and policy studies in the Graduate School of Education, University of California, Los Angeles.

Index

A

Aid to Families with Dependent Children (AFDC), 32, 33, 34, 35, 38, 39, 40, 41, 46
Alkin, M. C., 86, 96
Andersen, D. F., 87, 96
Auto workers, job retraining and placement strategies for, 5-29, 100-101

B

BASF plant, and job retraining program, 5, 14-19, 21-23, 28
Baumol, W., 54, 67
Berman, P., 85, 96
Birnbaum, M., 67
Boan, J., 81
Boston, mental health capital costs in, 75-80
Braskamp, L. A., 86, 96
Bui, X. T., 57, 67

C

Cannon, N. L., 2, 69-82, 102-103
Capital costs: accounting versus economic, 70-71; analysis of calculating, 69-82, 102-103; background on, 69-70; case study of, 75-80; conclusions on, 81; in cost-benefit study, 71-73; and market characteristics and price, 77-78; measurement methods for, 73-75; and opportunity cost, 73; and rental rates, 78-80; stock and flow measures in, 74; valuation procedure for, 76-77
Carr, C., 86, 96
Cassell, W., 71, 81
Catterall, J. S., 1-3, 99-103
Chambers, D. L., 32, 44, 51
Chase, S., 54, 67
Cheever, J., 85, 96
Child support: analysis of economic evaluation of, 31-51, 101-102; background on, 31-32; before-after and cross-site design for, 42-43; classical experimental design for, 40, 42; current weaknesses in, 32-34; data for, 39-40; demonstration on, 35-38; evaluation design for, 40-43; goals and constraints for, 34; and length of demonstration, 43-44; lessons in, 38-39; new and old cases of, 45; recommendations for, 34; sample nature and size for, 45-50; savings in, 34-35; statistical analysis of, 50-51
Chrysler assembly plant, and job retraining program, 11, 13, 14, 19-21
Chrysler foundry, and job retraining program, 14-17, 19-21
Cohen, J., 62, 67
Cohen, P., 62, 67
Comprehensive Employment and Training Act (CETA) of 1963, 6
Corbett, T., 2, 31-51, 101-102
Cost analysis: approaches in, 83-97, 103; background on, 83-84; conclusion on, 95-96; by evaluation contracting firm, 87-88; expectations for, 91-92; impediments to, 91, 93-95; literature review on, 86-87; national survey on, 89-96; need for, 84-85; purposes of, 89-90; types of, 85-86
Cost-benefit analysis, 85, 86, 90, 92
Cost-effectiveness analysis, 86-87, 90, 91, 92, 93-95, 96, 103
Cost-feasibility analysis, 85, 90, 91, 92
Cost-utility analysis, 85, 90, 91, 92

D

DANA plant, and job retraining program, 5, 14-19, 21-23, 28
Danziger, S., 32, 51
Davenport, B., 82
Detroit, job retraining and placement strategies in, 5-29
Dickey, B., 2, 69-82, 102-103
Downriver Community Conference, job retraining and placment strategies of, 5-29
Draper, N. R., 62, 67

E

Eckhardt, K., 44, 51
Economic evaluation: and capital costs, 69-82, 102-103; of child support demonstration, 31-51, 101-102; conclusions on, 99-103; cost analysis in, 83-97, 103; of job retraining and placement strategies, 5-29, 100-101; and nonmonetary benefits, 53-68, 102
Economics, commonalities of, with program evaluation, 1-2, 99-100
Education Consolidation and Improvement Act of 1981, 85
Edwards, W., 54, 57, 68

F

Finkler, S., 69, 81
Firestone Tire and Rubber plant, 5
Florio, D., 97
Ford Motor Company Michigan Casting plant, and job retraining program, 5, 11, 13, 14, 19 23, 24, 26, 28
Fullen, M., 85, 96

G

Garfinkel, I., 2, 31-51, 101-102
Garms, W., 84, 96
Gramlich, E., 58, 68
Gray, P. J., 85, 96
Grether, D., 57, 68
Grunberg, F., 81
Guilford, J. P., 59, 65, 68

H

Hartman, W. T., 87, 96
Harvard University, Medical School of, 76
Hendrickson, L. S., 87, 97
Henerson, M., 59, 68
Hilton, G., 62, 68

I

Institute for Research on Poverty (IRP), 31

J

Job retraining and placement strategies: analysis of economic evaluation of, 5-29, 100-101; background on, 5-6; comparison group in, 10-11; conclusions on, 27-29; data sources and analysis sample for, 13-14; design elements in, 7-9; differences adjusted in, 11-13; and employment and earnings overview, 14-21; external validity of, 28-29; first phase effects of, 15-19; impacts and implications of, 21-24; internal validity of, 23-24, 28; outcome variable measurement in, 9-10; participation in, 6-7; program effects of, 9-14; program service effects of, 24-27; second phase effects of, 19-21; and selection bias, 11

K

Keeney, R., 54, 68
Kirst, M., 84, 96
Klees, S. J., 86, 96
Kucic, A. R., 71, 81
Kulik, J., 2, 5-29, 100-101

L

Lear-Siegler plant, and job retraining program, 14-17
Levin, H. M., 84, 85, 86, 96
Lewis, D., 65, 68
Lorenzen, G. L., 86, 96

M

McGuire, T., 2, 69-82, 102-103
McLaughlin, M. W., 85, 96
Madison, Wisconsin, mental health cost-benefit study in, 71-73
Massachusetts: Department of Mental Health in, 76; mental health capital costs in, 75-80
Massachusetts Mental Health Center (MMHC), capital costs at, 75-80
May, P., 71, 81
Melli, M., 31, 51
Mendota Mental Health Institute, cost-benefit study at, 71-73
Mental health services, capital costs of, 69-82, 102-103
Michigan: Genessee County in, 44; job retraining and placement strategies in, 5-29; unemployment insurance in, 10

107

Mishan, E., 58, 68
Mosher, L. R., 69, 81
Moynihan, D. P., 34, 51
Mullin, S. P., 87, 96

N

Nagel, S., 3, 53-68, 102
National Institute of Education, 83n
Newman, R., 54, 57, 68
Nonmonetary benefits: analysis of calculating, 53-68, 102; background on, 53-54; conclusions on, 66-67; and diminishing returns, 60-63; incremental analysis for, 54, 56, 57, 66; method alternatives for, 57-58; paired-comparison method for, 54, 58-60, 66-67; percentaging analysis for, 56-57, 66; problem of, 54-58; and relevant decision makers, 58-59; and threshold equation transformation, 60-63; turning point in, 54; variations in method for, 63-66
Northwest Regional Educational Laboratory, 83n

P

Page, E. B., 85, 96
Phillips, L., 59, 68
Political science, concept of, 53
Pomfret, A., 85, 96
Prell, A., 59, 68
Program evaluation, commonalities of, with economics, 1-2, 99-100. *See also* Economic evaluation

Q

Quinn, B., 86, 96

R

Raiffa, H., 54, 68
Reagan administration, 102
Rhoads, S., 54, 68
Rose, A., 59, 68
Rubin, J., 69, 81

S

Saaty, T., 54, 57, 68
Sellin, T., 54, 59, 68

Sikorski, L., 97
Smith, C., 81
Smith, D. A., 2, 5-29, 100-101
Smith, H., 62, 67
Smith, J. K., 3, 83-97, 103
Smith, M. C., 87, 97
Smith, N. L., 3, 83-97, 103
Solmon, L. C., 86, 96
Sorensen, J., 71, 81
Stanfield, J., 85, 97
Stein, L., 82
Stokey, E., 67, 68
Stone, A., 82
Stromsdorfer, E. W., 2, 5-29, 100-101
Sugden, R., 58, 68, 79, 81
Sullivan, J. M., 85, 97
Summers, A. A., 87, 96
Supplemental Unemployment Benefits (SUB), 10

T

Test, M. A., 82
Thomas, P., 81
Thompson, M. S., 54, 58, 86, 97
Trade Readjustment Assistance (TRA), 10, 22
Tufte, E., 65, 68

U

U.S. Department of Commerce, 32, 51
U.S. Department of Health and Human Services, 58, 60
U.S. Department of Labor, 5

V

Votey, H., 59, 68
Vraciw, R. A., 70, 81

W

Wargo, M. J., 87, 97
Weisbrod, B., 72, 75, 82
Wells, S. J., 86, 96
White, M., 67, 68
Wholeben, B. E., 85, 97
Wilde, L., 57, 68
Williams, A., 58, 68, 79, 81

Wisconsin: child support demonstration in, 31-51; Dane County in, 44; Department of Health and Social Services (DHSS) in, 31, 37; Department of Revenue in, 38; mental health cost-benefit study in, 71-73
Wisconsin Survey Lab, 47
Wolfgang, M., 54, 59, 68
Wortman, P. M., 83, 97

Y

Yee, L. M., 32, 51

Z

Zaltman, G., 97
Zeckhauser, R., 67, 68
Zeleny, M., 57, 68
Zelman, W., 71, 82